STORYBOARD 16:9 CINEMA NOTEBOOK

VISUAL STORYTELLING TECHNOLOGY

100 PAGE NOTEBOOK

THE PRODUCTIVE LUDDITE™

PAPER. PRODUCTIVITY. CREATIVITY. BETTER LIVING.

VITAL INFORMATION

THIS NOTEBOOK IS OWNED & OPERATED BY

IS THIS NOTEBOOK LOST?
PLEASE RETURN TO / PLEASE CONTACT

REWARD: ○ **THE WARM FEELING OF DOING GOOD**
○ **COLD HARD CASH $**_______________
○ **ALL OF THE ABOVE**

START DATE   **END DATE**

SUBJECT MATTER   **VOLUME / ID#**

SUMMARY / ABSTRACT

The Productive Luddite is a brand celebrating paper-based technologies — books, notebooks, diaries, and journals — that help you transform the complexity of modern living into simplicity, simplicity into productivity, and productivity into creativity and better living.

If you like **STORYBOARD 16:9 CINEMA NOTEBOOK**, you may also enjoy using: **Storyboard Thumbnails 16:9 Cinema, Storyboard 4:3 TV, Storyboard 1.85:1 Movie, Storyboard 2.39:1 Theatre, Storyboard Thumbnails 4:3 TV, Storyboard Thumbnails 1.85:1 Movie, Storyboard Thumbnails 2.39:1 Theatre.**

© 2010 Productive Luddite
All Rights Reserved.
Printed in the United States, ironically, by machines.
Designed in Canada.
ISBN: 978-1-926892-34-4

Do you have any suggestions for improving this product or any of The Productive Luddite's products? Please send email to: info@productiveluddite.com.

TITLE:
DATE
PAGE
SCENE
SHOT
NO.
SCENE
SHOT
NO.
SCENE
SHOT
NO.
SCENE
SHOT
NO.

TITLE:
DATE
PAGE
SCENE
SHOT
NO.
SCENE
SHOT
NO.
SCENE
SHOT
NO.
SCENE
SHOT
NO.

TITLE:
DATE
PAGE
SCENE
SHOT
NO.
SCENE
SHOT
NO.
SCENE
SHOT
NO.
SCENE
SHOT
NO.

TITLE:
DATE
PAGE
SCENE
SHOT
NO.
SCENE
SHOT
NO.
SCENE
SHOT
NO.
SCENE
SHOT
NO.

TITLE:
DATE
PAGE
SCENE
SHOT
NO.
SCENE
SHOT
NO.
SCENE
SHOT
NO.
SCENE
SHOT
NO.

TITLE:
DATE
PAGE
SCENE
SHOT
NO.
SCENE
SHOT
NO.
SCENE
SHOT
NO.
SCENE
SHOT
NO.

TITLE:

DATE

PAGE

SCENE   SHOT   NO.

SCENE   SHOT   NO.

SCENE   SHOT   NO.

SCENE   SHOT   NO.

TITLE:
DATE
PAGE
SCENE
SHOT
NO.
SCENE
SHOT
NO.
SCENE
SHOT
NO.
SCENE
SHOT
NO.

TITLE:
DATE
PAGE
SCENE
SHOT
NO.
SCENE
SHOT
NO.
SCENE
SHOT
NO.
SCENE
SHOT
NO.

TITLE:
DATE
PAGE
SCENE
SHOT
NO.
SCENE
SHOT
NO.
SCENE
SHOT
NO.
SCENE
SHOT
NO.

TITLE:
DATE
PAGE
SCENE
SHOT
NO.
SCENE
SHOT
NO.
SCENE
SHOT
NO.
SCENE
SHOT
NO.

TITLE:
DATE
PAGE
SCENE
SHOT
NO.
SCENE
SHOT
NO.
SCENE
SHOT
NO.
SCENE
SHOT
NO.

TITLE:
DATE
PAGE
SCENE
SHOT
NO.
SCENE
SHOT
NO.
SCENE
SHOT
NO.
SCENE
SHOT
NO.

TITLE:
DATE
PAGE
SCENE
SHOT
NO.
SCENE
SHOT
NO.
SCENE
SHOT
NO.
SCENE
SHOT
NO.

TITLE:
DATE
PAGE
SCENE
SHOT
NO.
SCENE
SHOT
NO.
SCENE
SHOT
NO.
SCENE
SHOT
NO.

TITLE:
DATE
PAGE
SCENE
SHOT
NO.
SCENE
SHOT
NO.
SCENE
SHOT
NO.
SCENE
SHOT
NO.

TITLE:
DATE
PAGE
SCENE
SHOT
NO.
SCENE
SHOT
NO.
SCENE
SHOT
NO.
SCENE
SHOT
NO.

TITLE:
DATE
PAGE
SCENE
SHOT
NO.
SCENE
SHOT
NO.
SCENE
SHOT
NO.
SCENE
SHOT
NO.

TITLE:
DATE
PAGE
SCENE
SHOT
NO.
SCENE
SHOT
NO.
SCENE
SHOT
NO.
SCENE
SHOT
NO.

TITLE:
DATE
PAGE
SCENE
SHOT
NO.
SCENE
SHOT
NO.
SCENE
SHOT
NO.
SCENE
SHOT
NO.

TITLE:
DATE
PAGE
SCENE
SHOT
NO.
SCENE
SHOT
NO.
SCENE
SHOT
NO.
SCENE
SHOT
NO.

TITLE:
DATE
PAGE
SCENE
SHOT
NO.
SCENE
SHOT
NO.
SCENE
SHOT
NO.
SCENE
SHOT
NO.

TITLE:
DATE
PAGE
SCENE
SHOT
NO.
SCENE
SHOT
NO.
SCENE
SHOT
NO.
SCENE
SHOT
NO.

TITLE:
DATE
PAGE
SCENE
SHOT
NO.
SCENE
SHOT
NO.
SCENE
SHOT
NO.
SCENE
SHOT
NO.

TITLE:
DATE
PAGE
SCENE
SHOT
NO.
SCENE
SHOT
NO.
SCENE
SHOT
NO.
SCENE
SHOT
NO.

TITLE:
DATE
PAGE
SCENE
SHOT
NO.
SCENE
SHOT
NO.
SCENE
SHOT
NO.
SCENE
SHOT
NO.

TITLE:
DATE
PAGE
SCENE
SHOT
NO.
SCENE
SHOT
NO.
SCENE
SHOT
NO.
SCENE
SHOT
NO.

TITLE:
DATE
PAGE
SCENE
SHOT
NO.
SCENE
SHOT
NO.
SCENE
SHOT
NO.
SCENE
SHOT
NO.

TITLE:
DATE
PAGE
SCENE
SHOT
NO.
SCENE
SHOT
NO.
SCENE
SHOT
NO
SCENE
SHOT
NO.

TITLE:
DATE
PAGE
SCENE
SHOT
NO.
SCENE
SHOT
NO.
SCENE
SHOT
NO.
SCENE
SHOT
NO.

TITLE:
DATE
PAGE
SCENE
SHOT
NO.
SCENE
SHOT
NO.
SCENE
SHOT
NO.
SCENE
SHOT
NO.

TITLE:
DATE
PAGE
SCENE
SHOT
NO.
SCENE
SHOT
NO.
SCENE
SHOT
NO.
SCENE
SHOT
NO.

TITLE:
DATE
PAGE
SCENE
SHOT
NO.
SCENE
SHOT
NO.
SCENE
SHOT
NO.
SCENE
SHOT
NO.

TITLE:
DATE
PAGE
SCENE
SHOT
NO.
SCENE
SHOT
NO.
SCENE
SHOT
NO.
SCENE
SHOT
NO.

TITLE:
DATE
PAGE
SCENE
SHOT
NO.
SCENE
SHOT
NO.
SCENE
SHOT
NO.
SCENE
SHOT
NO.

TITLE:
DATE
PAGE
SCENE
SHOT
NO.
SCENE
SHOT
NO.
SCENE
SHOT
NO.
SCENE
SHOT
NO.

TITLE:
DATE
PAGE
SCENE
SHOT
NO.
SCENE
SHOT
NO.
SCENE
SHOT
NO.
SCENE
SHOT
NO.

TITLE:
DATE
PAGE
SCENE
SHOT
NO.
SCENE
SHOT
NO.
SCENE
SHOT
NO.
SCENE
SHOT
NO.

TITLE:
DATE
PAGE
SCENE
SHOT
NO.
SCENE
SHOT
NO.
SCENE
SHOT
NO.
SCENE
SHOT
NO.

TITLE:
DATE
PAGE
SCENE
SHOT
NO.
SCENE
SHOT
NO.
SCENE
SHOT
NO.
SCENE
SHOT
NO.

TITLE:
DATE
PAGE
SCENE
SHOT
NO.
SCENE
SHOT
NO.
SCENE
SHOT
NO.
SCENE
SHOT
NO.

TITLE:
DATE
PAGE
SCENE
SHOT
NO.
SCENE
SHOT
NO.
SCENE
SHOT
NO.
SCENE
SHOT
NO.

TITLE:
DATE
PAGE
SCENE
SHOT
NO.
SCENE
SHOT
NO.
SCENE
SHOT
NO.
SCENE
SHOT
NO.

TITLE:
DATE
PAGE
SCENE
SHOT
NO.
SCENE
SHOT
NO.
SCENE
SHOT
NO.
SCENE
SHOT
NO.

TITLE:
DATE
PAGE
SCENE
SHOT
NO.
SCENE
SHOT
NO.
SCENE
SHOT
NO.
SCENE
SHOT
NO.

TITLE:
DATE
PAGE
SCENE
SHOT
NO.
SCENE
SHOT
NO.
SCENE
SHOT
NO.
SCENE
SHOT
NO.

TITLE:
DATE
PAGE
SCENE
SHOT
NO.
SCENE
SHOT
NO.
SCENE
SHOT
NO.
SCENE
SHOT
NO.

TITLE:
DATE
PAGE
SCENE
SHOT
NO.
SCENE
SHOT
NO.
SCENE
SHOT
NO.
SCENE
SHOT
NO.

TITLE:
DATE
PAGE
SCENE
SHOT
NO.
SCENE
SHOT
NO.
SCENE
SHOT
NO.
SCENE
SHOT
NO.

TITLE:
DATE
PAGE
SCENE
SHOT
NO.
SCENE
SHOT
NO.
SCENE
SHOT
NO.
SCENE
SHOT
NO.

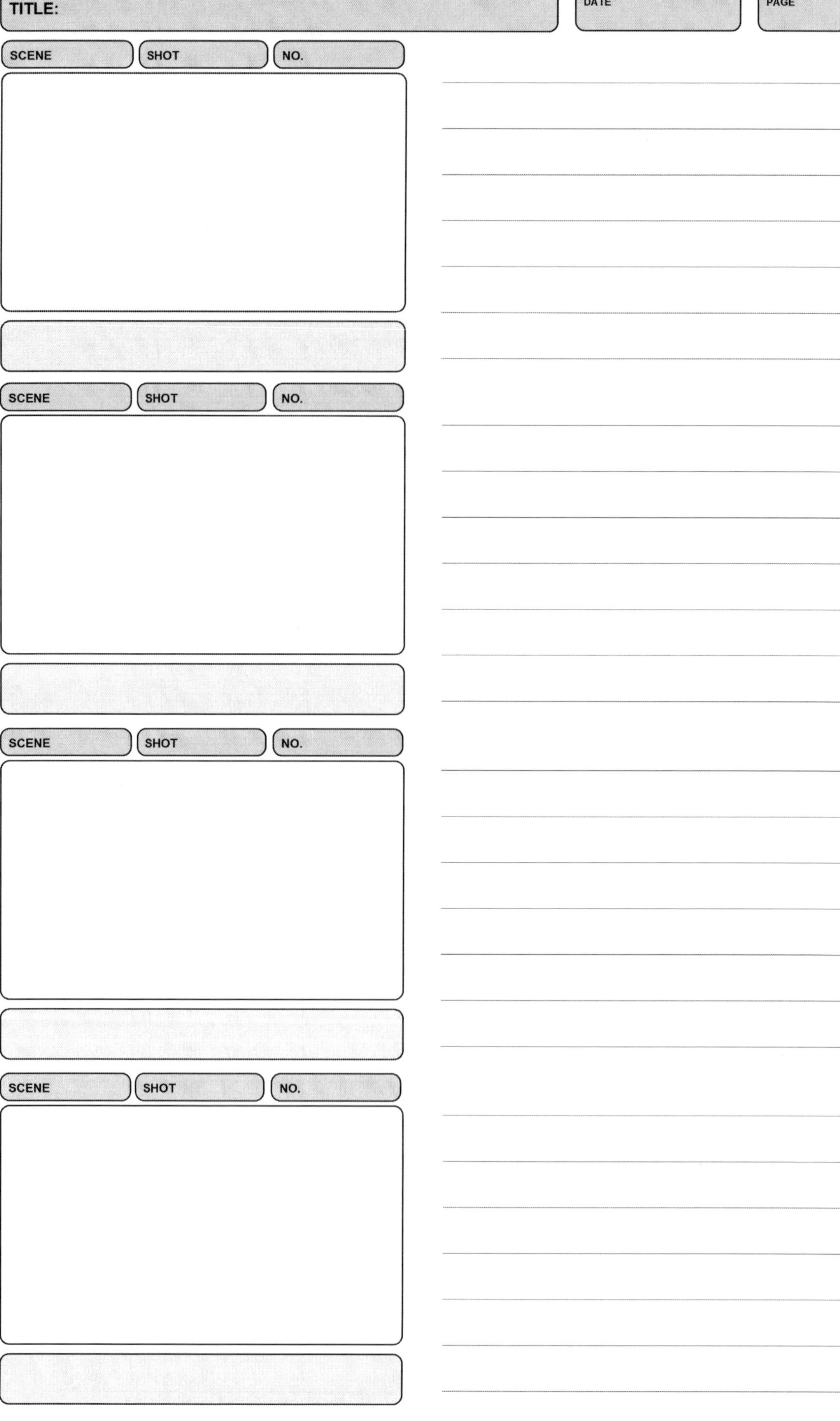

TITLE:
DATE
PAGE
SCENE
SHOT
NO.
SCENE
SHOT
NO.
SCENE
SHOT
NO.
SCENE
SHOT
NO.

TITLE:
DATE
PAGE
SCENE
SHOT
NO.
SCENE
SHOT
NO.
SCENE
SHOT
NO.
SCENE
SHOT
NO.

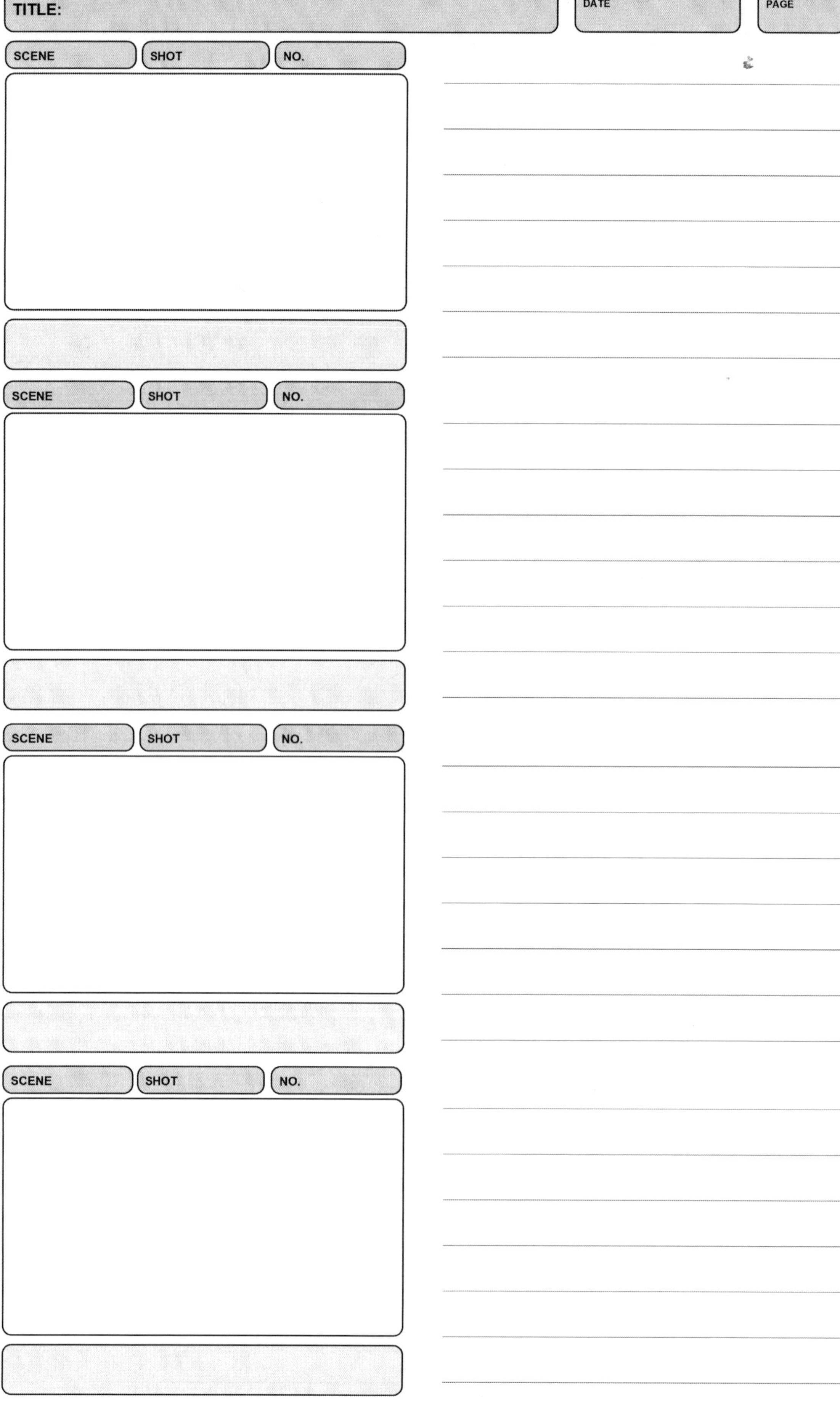

TITLE:
DATE
PAGE
SCENE
SHOT
NO.
SCENE
SHOT
NO.
SCENE
SHOT
NO.
SCENE
SHOT
NO.

TITLE:
DATE
PAGE
SCENE
SHOT
NO.
SCENE
SHOT
NO.
SCENE
SHOT
NO.
SCENE
SHOT
NO.

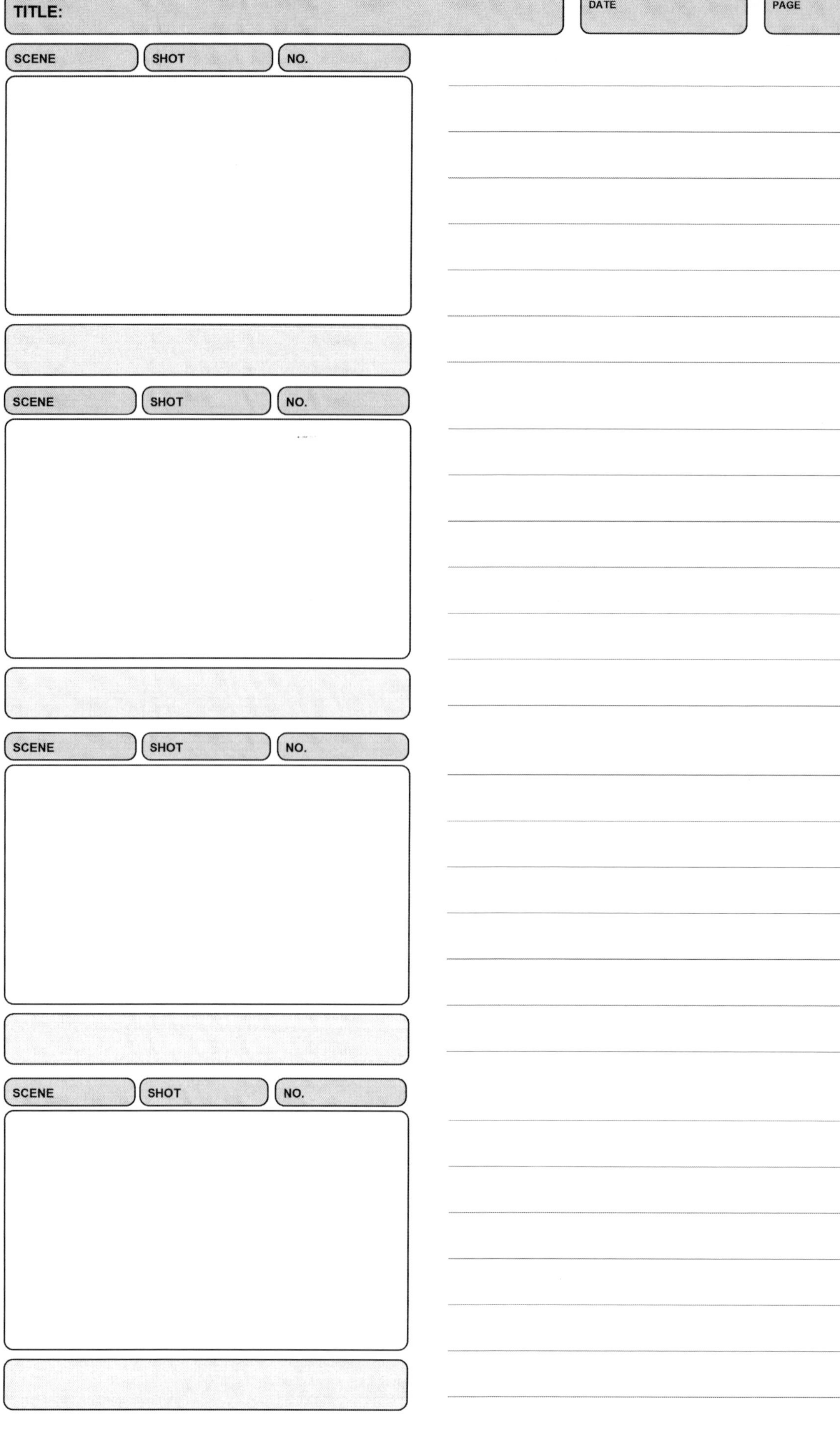

TITLE:
DATE
PAGE
SCENE
SHOT
NO.
SCENE
SHOT
NO.
SCENE
SHOT
NO.
SCENE
SHOT
NO.

TITLE:
DATE
PAGE
SCENE
SHOT
NO.
SCENE
SHOT
NO.
SCENE
SHOT
NO.
SCENE
SHOT
NO.

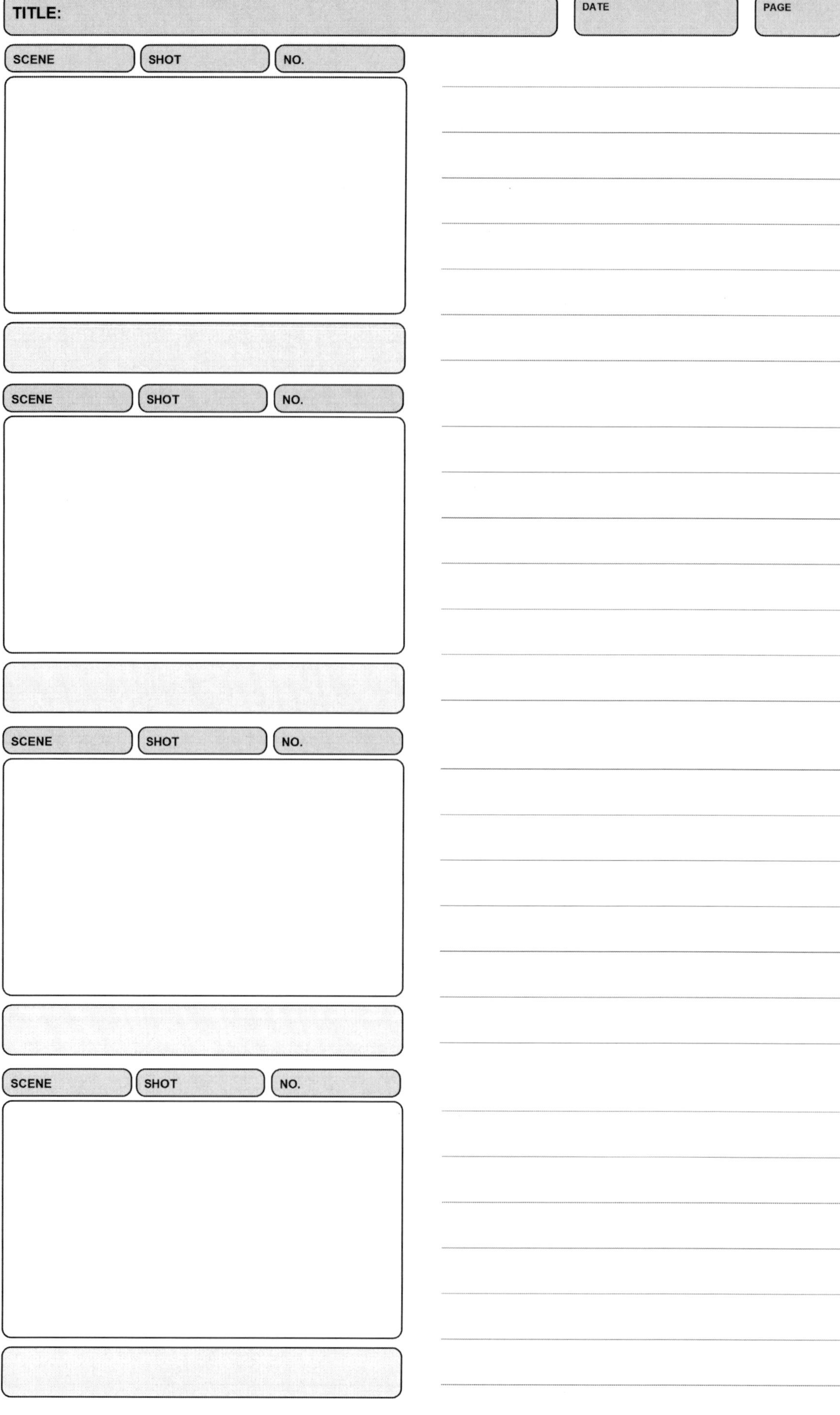
TITLE:
DATE
PAGE
SCENE
SHOT
NO.
SCENE
SHOT
NO.
SCENE
SHOT
NO.
SCENE
SHOT
NO.

TITLE:
DATE
PAGE
SCENE
SHOT
NO.
SCENE
SHOT
NO.
SCENE
SHOT
NO.
SCENE
SHOT
NO.

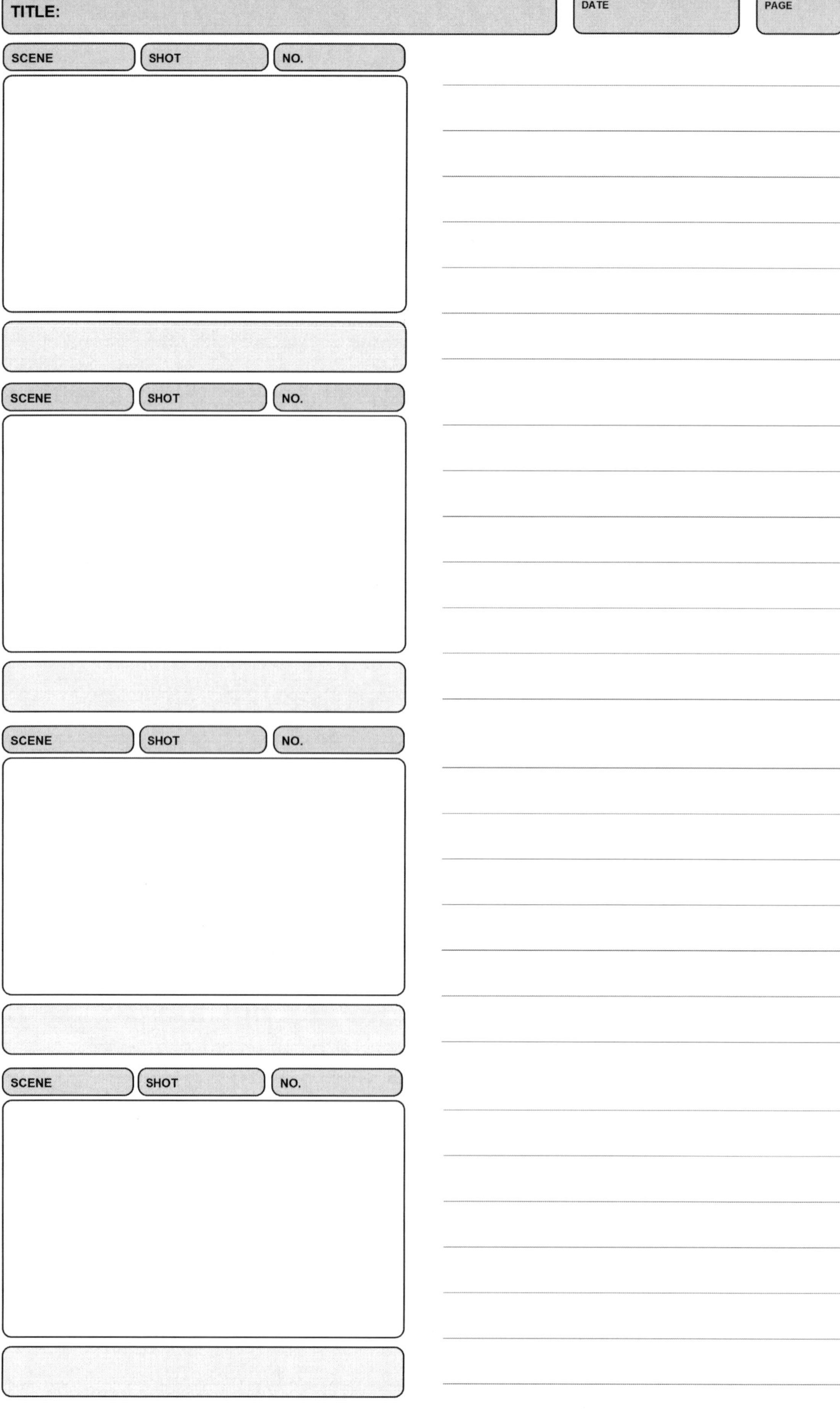

TITLE:
DATE
PAGE
SCENE
SHOT
NO.
SCENE
SHOT
NO.
SCENE
SHOT
NO.
SCENE
SHOT
NO.

TITLE:
DATE
PAGE
SCENE
SHOT
NO.
SCENE
SHOT
NO.
SCENE
SHOT
NO.
SCENE
SHOT
NO.

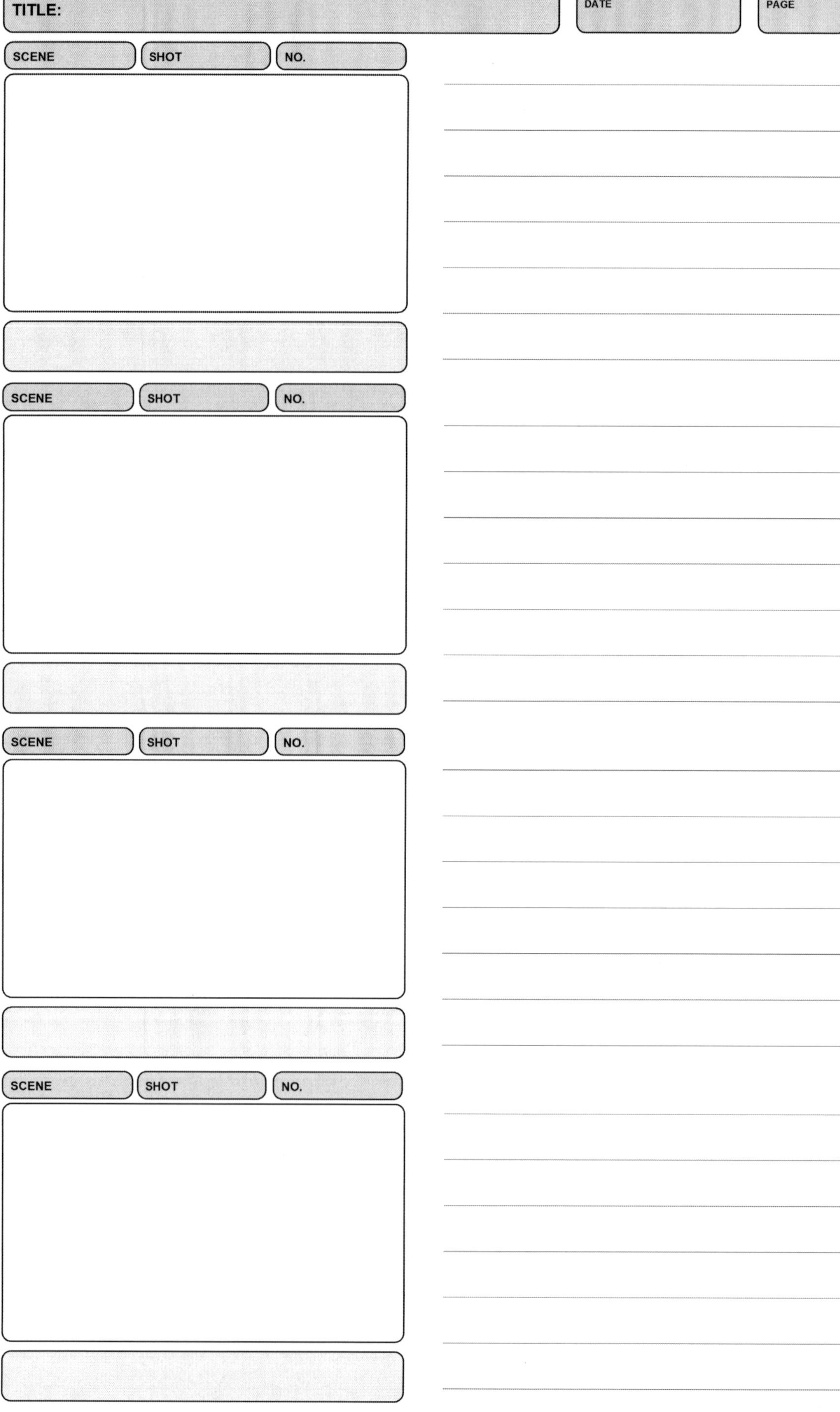

TITLE:
DATE
PAGE
SCENE
SHOT
NO.
SCENE
SHOT
NO.
SCENE
SHOT
NO.
SCENE
SHOT
NO.

TITLE:
DATE
PAGE
SCENE
SHOT
NO.
SCENE
SHOT
NO.
SCENE
SHOT
NO.
SCENE
SHOT
NO.

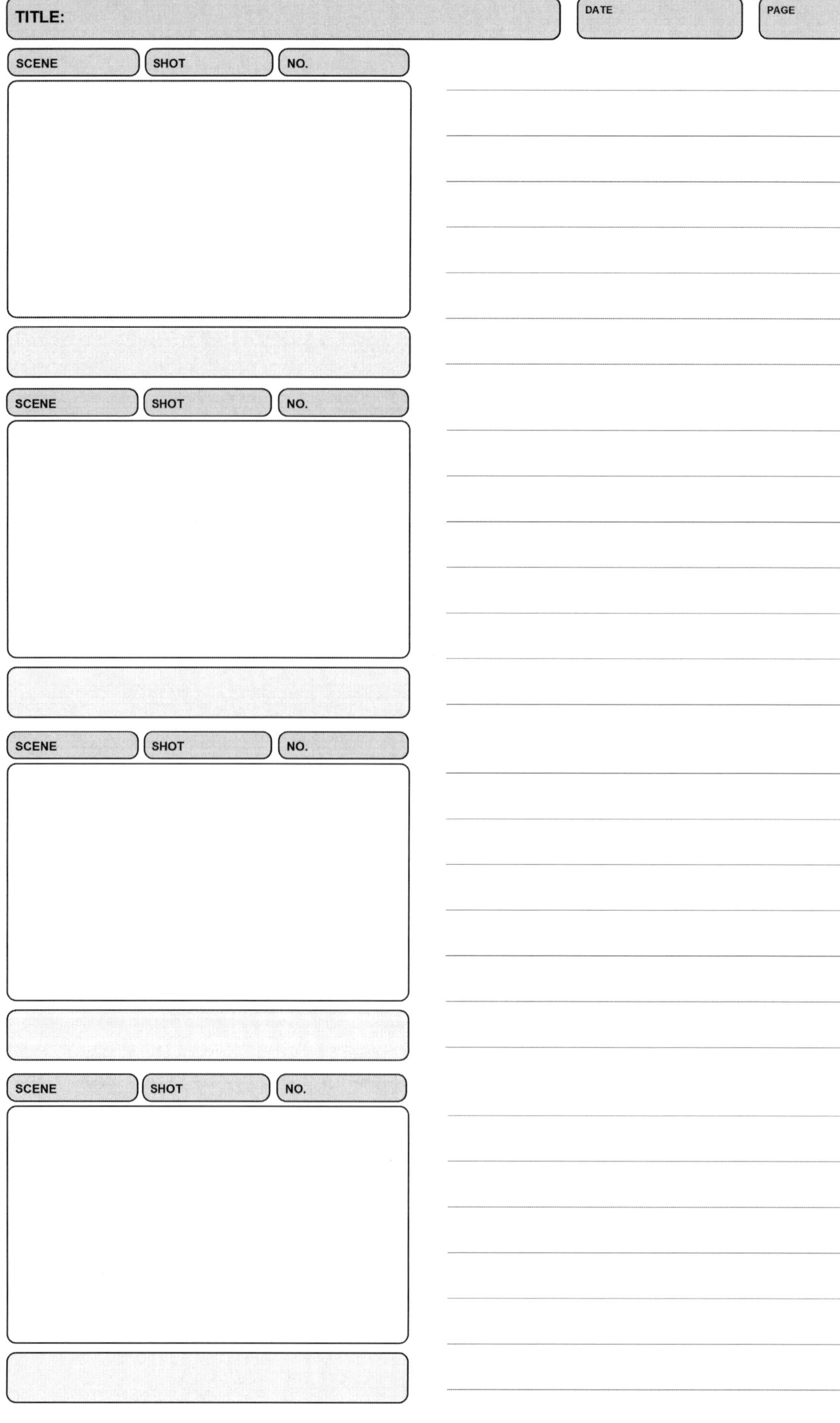

TITLE:
DATE
PAGE
SCENE
SHOT
NO.
SCENE
SHOT
NO.
SCENE
SHOT
NO.
SCENE
SHOT
NO.

TITLE:

DATE

PAGE

SCENE

SHOT

NO.

SCENE

SHOT

NO.

SCENE

SHOT

NO.

SCENE

SHOT

NO.

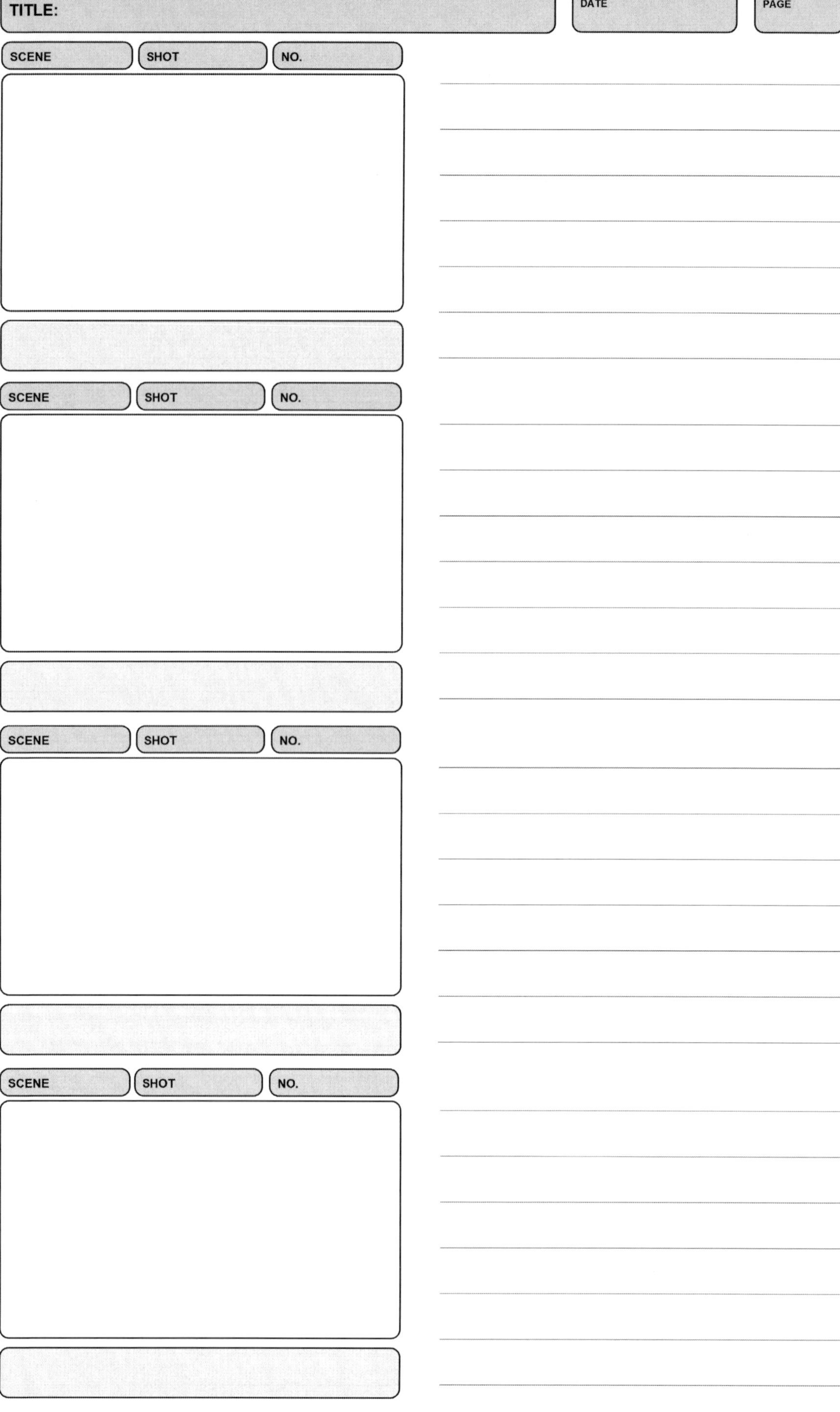
TITLE:
DATE
PAGE
SCENE
SHOT
NO.
SCENE
SHOT
NO.
SCENE
SHOT
NO.
SCENE
SHOT
NO.

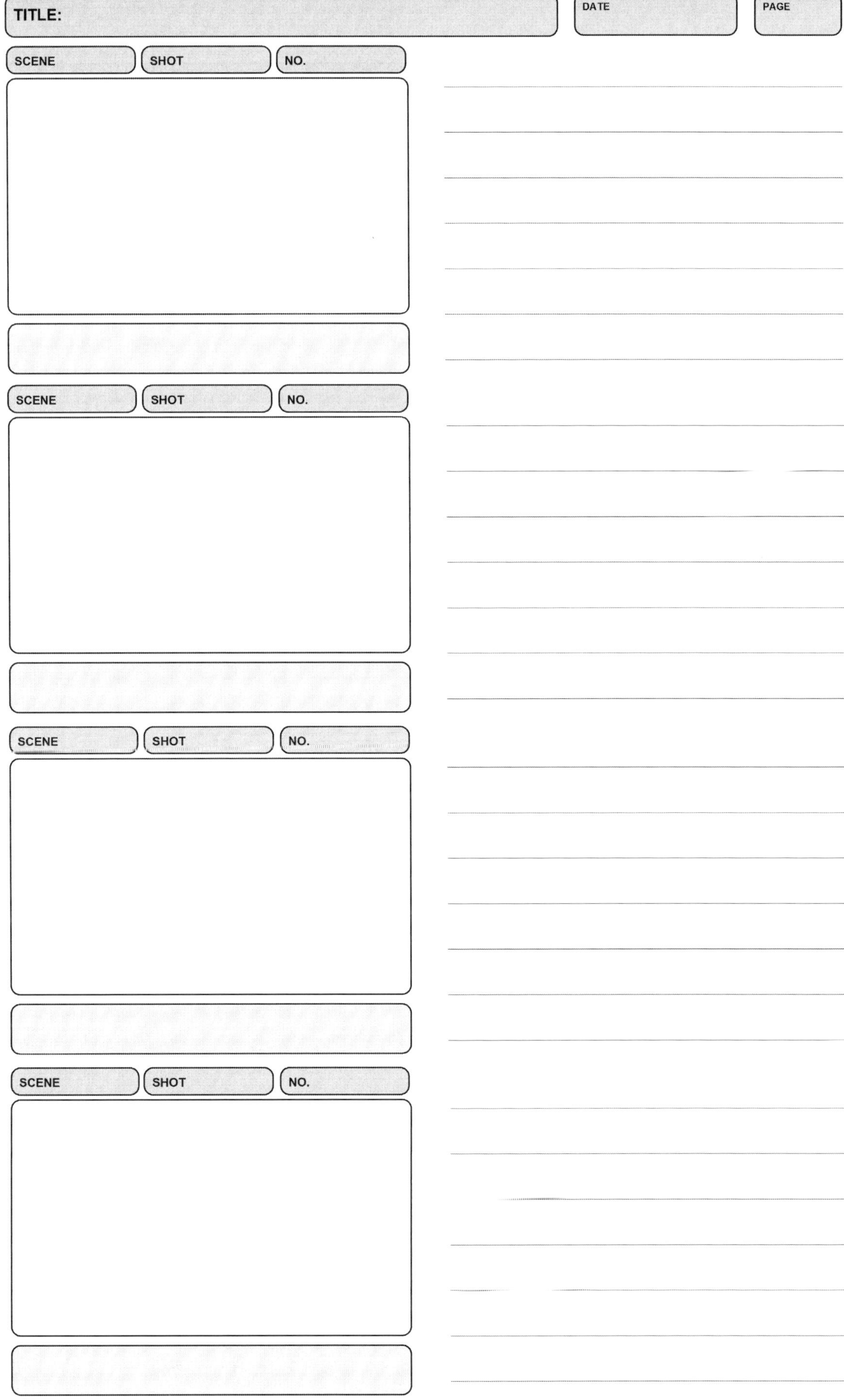

TITLE:
DATE
PAGE
SCENE
SHOT
NO.
SCENE
SHOT
NO.
SCENE
SHOT
NO.
SCENE
SHOT
NO.

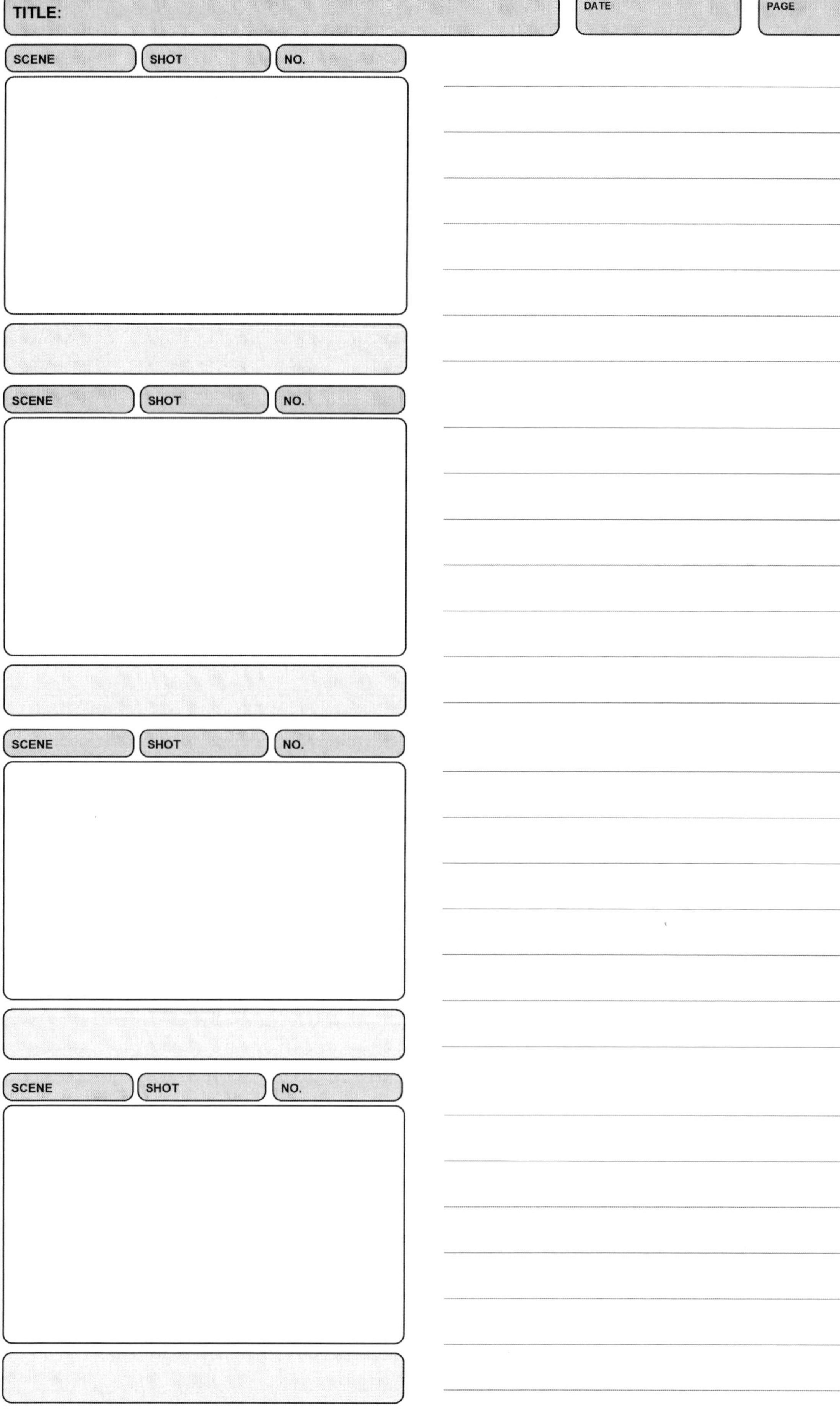

TITLE:
DATE
PAGE
SCENE
SHOT
NO.
SCENE
SHOT
NO.
SCENE
SHOT
NO.
SCENE
SHOT
NO.

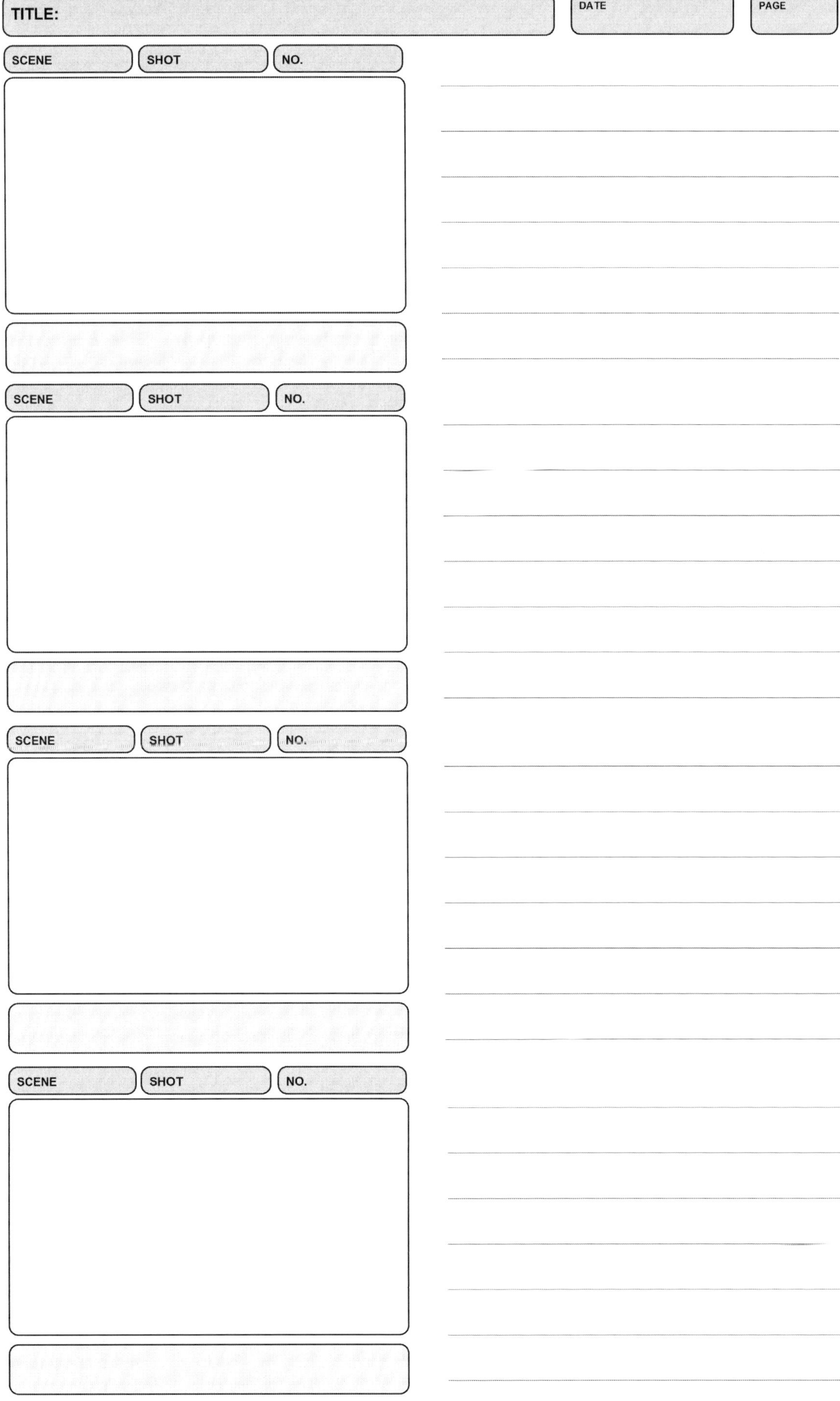
TITLE:
DATE
PAGE
SCENE
SHOT
NO.
SCENE
SHOT
NO.
SCENE
SHOT
NO.
SCENE
SHOT
NO.

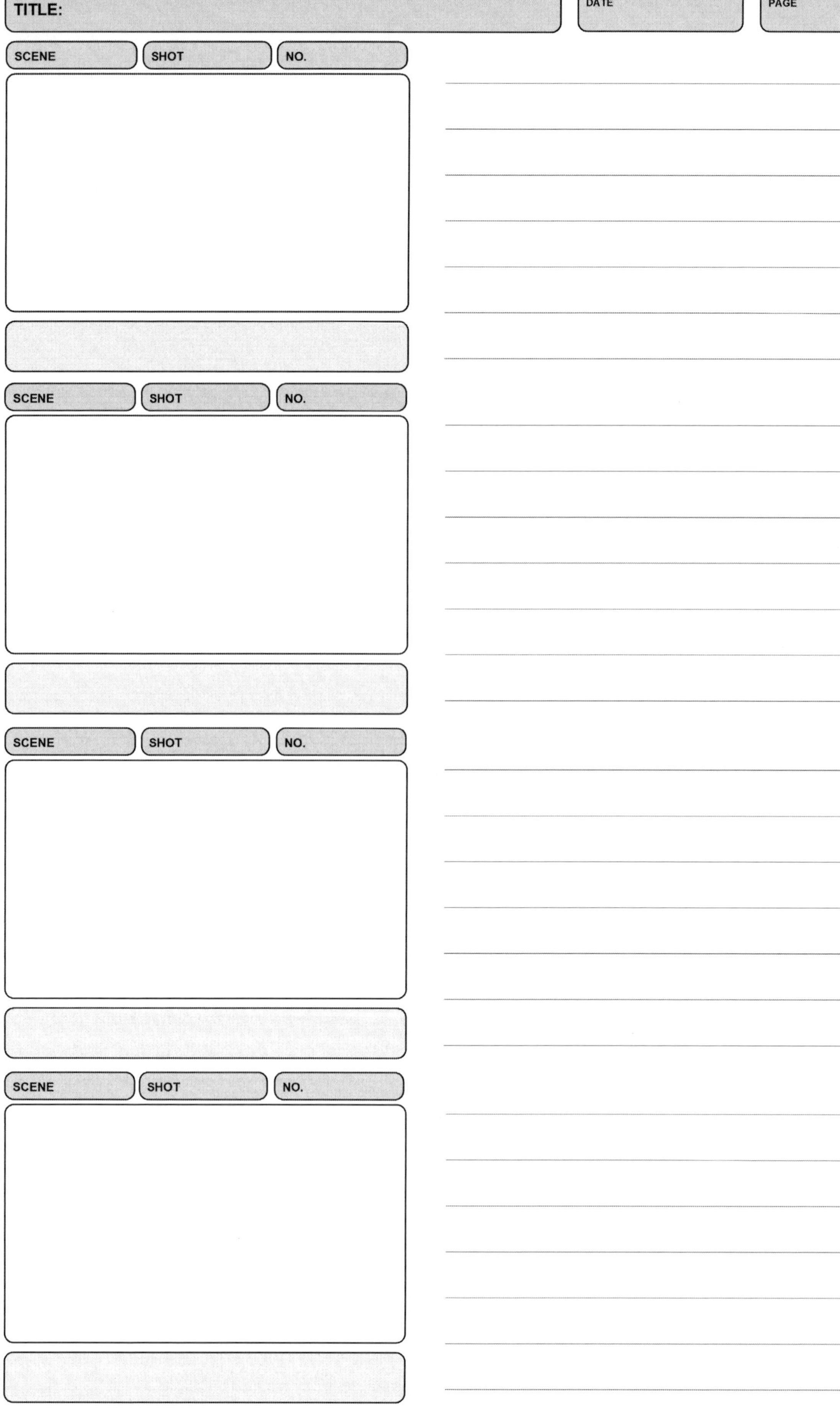

TITLE:
DATE
PAGE
SCENE
SHOT
NO.
SCENE
SHOT
NO.
SCENE
SHOT
NO.
SCENE
SHOT
NO.

TITLE:
DATE
PAGE
SCENE
SHOT
NO.
SCENE
SHOT
NO.
SCENE
SHOT
NO.
SCENE
SHOT
NO.

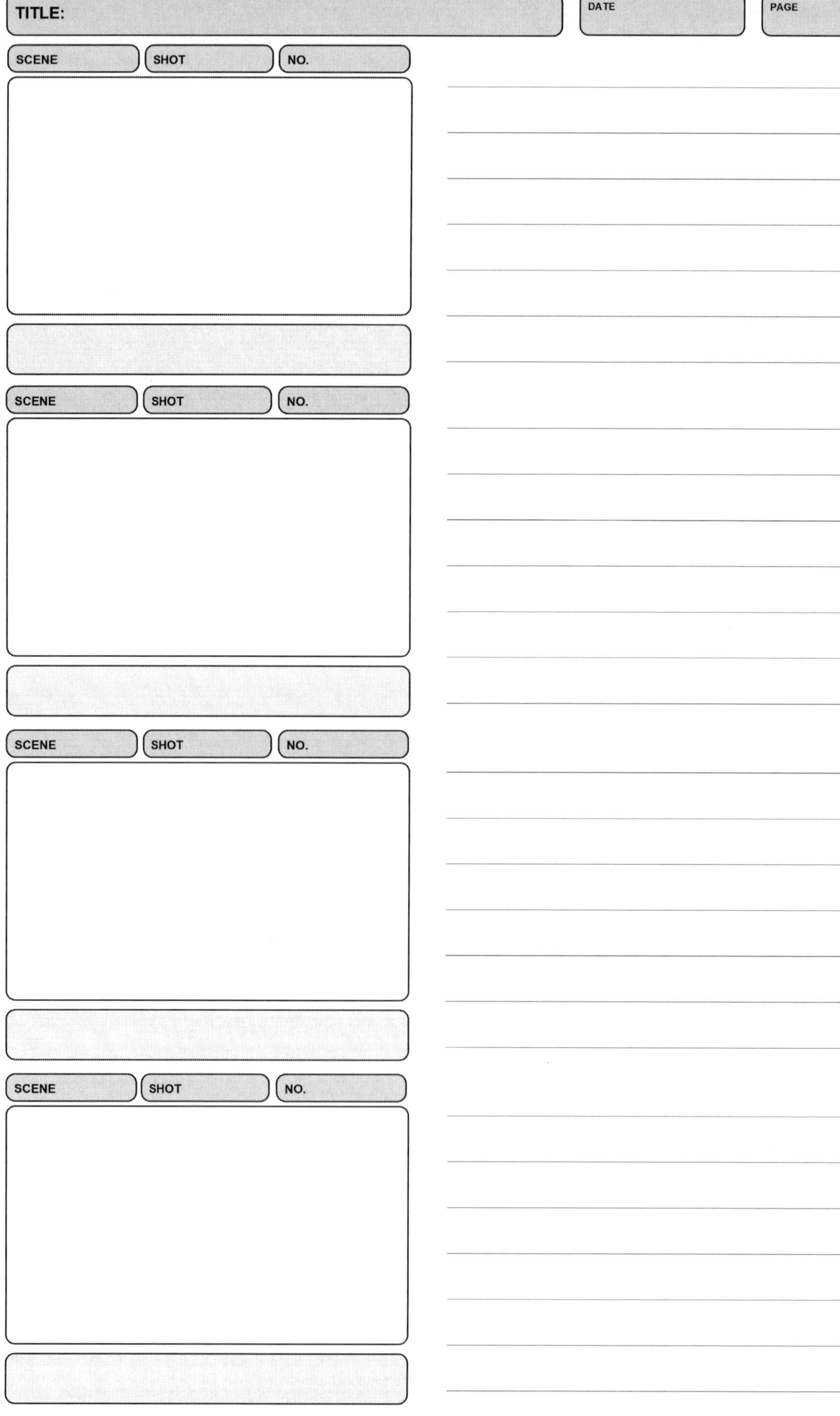

TITLE:
DATE
PAGE
SCENE
SHOT
NO.
SCENE
SHOT
NO.
SCENE
SHOT
NO.
SCENE
SHOT
NO.

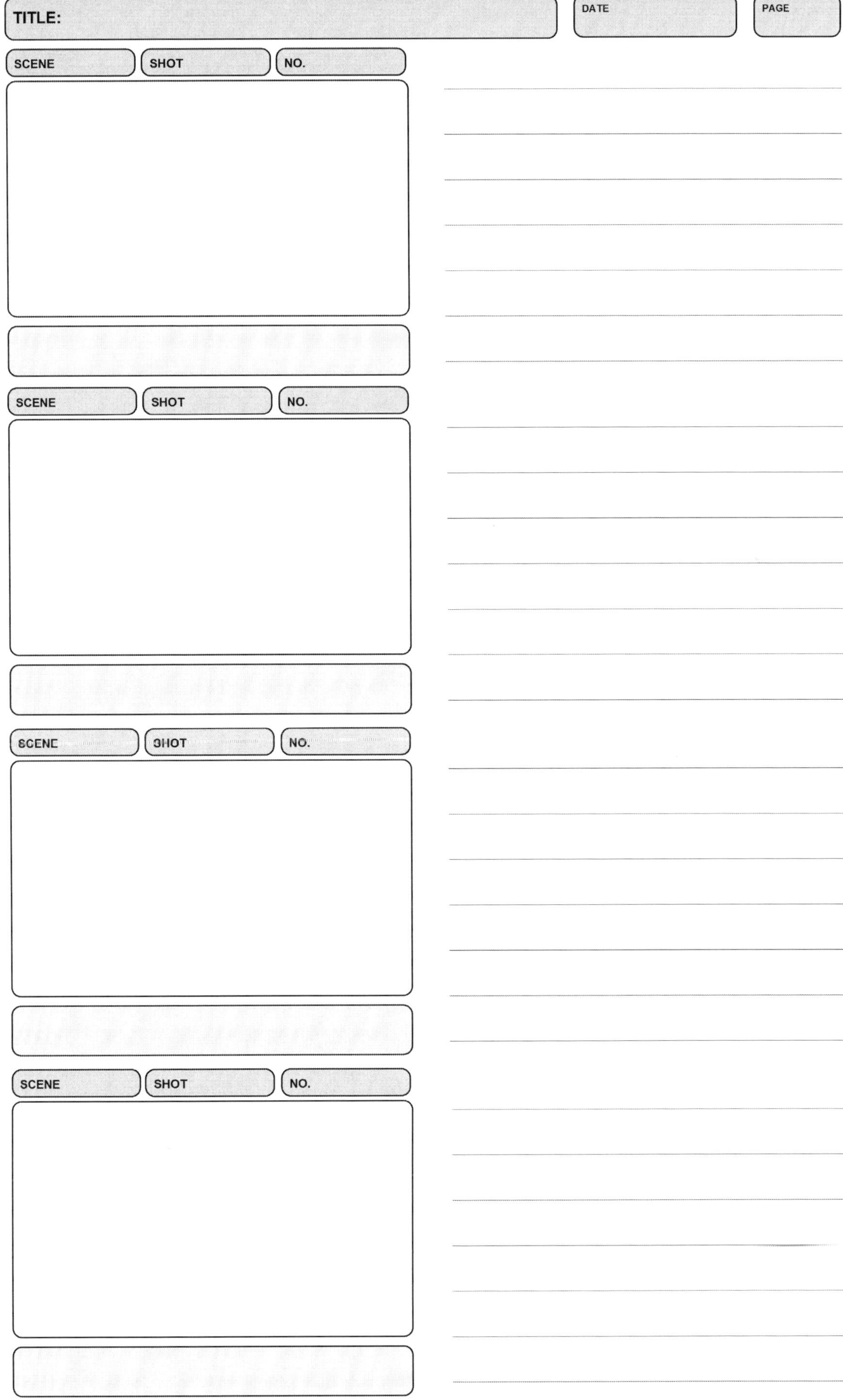
TITLE:
DATE
PAGE
SCENE
SHOT
NO.
SCENE
SHOT
NO.
SCENE
SHOT
NO.
SCENE
SHOT
NO.

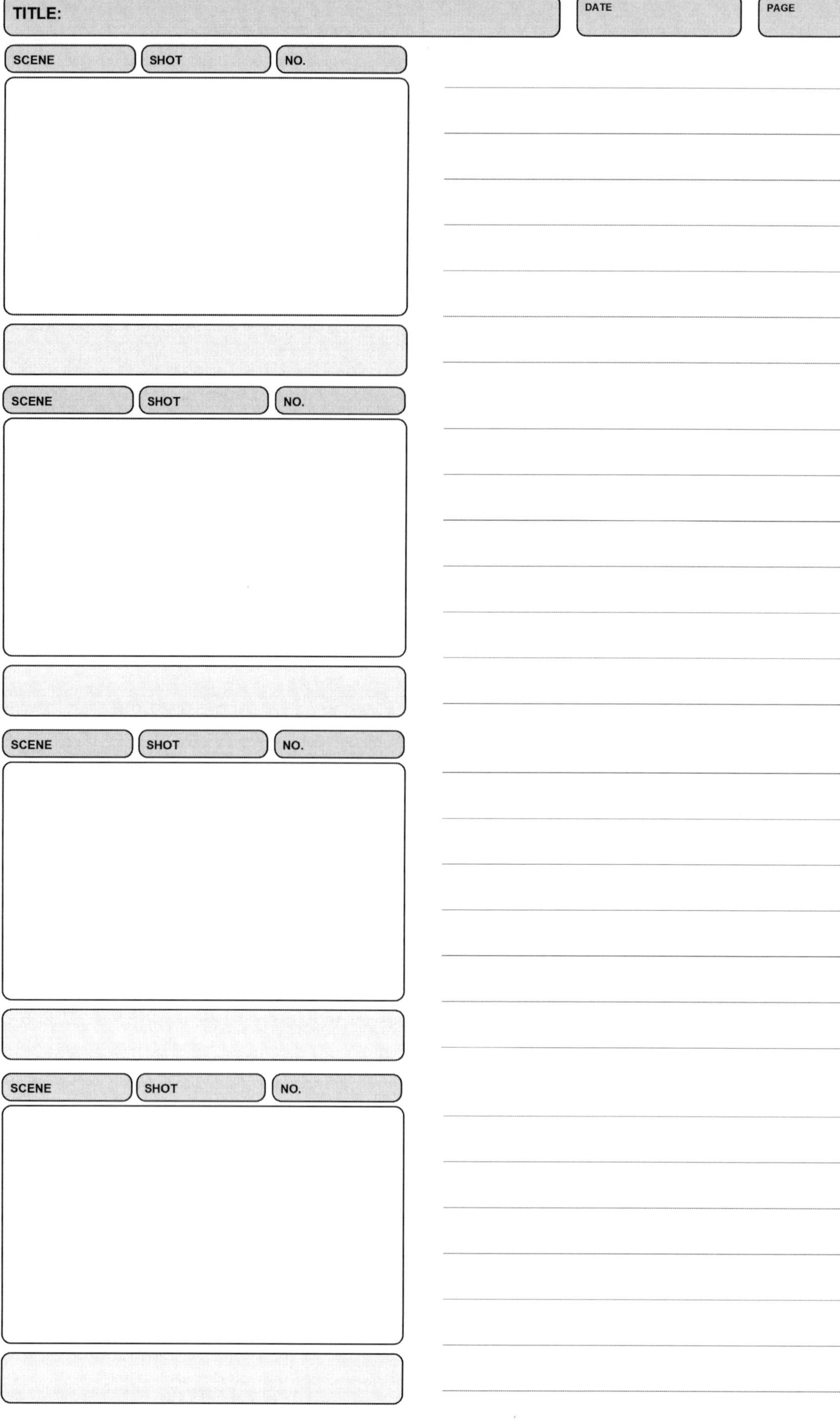

TITLE:
DATE
PAGE
SCENE
SHOT
NO.
SCENE
SHOT
NO.
SCENE
SHOT
NO.
SCENE
SHOT
NO.

TITLE:
DATE
PAGE
SCENE
SHOT
NO.
SCENE
SHOT
NO.
SCENE
SHOT
NO.
SCENE
SHOT
NO.

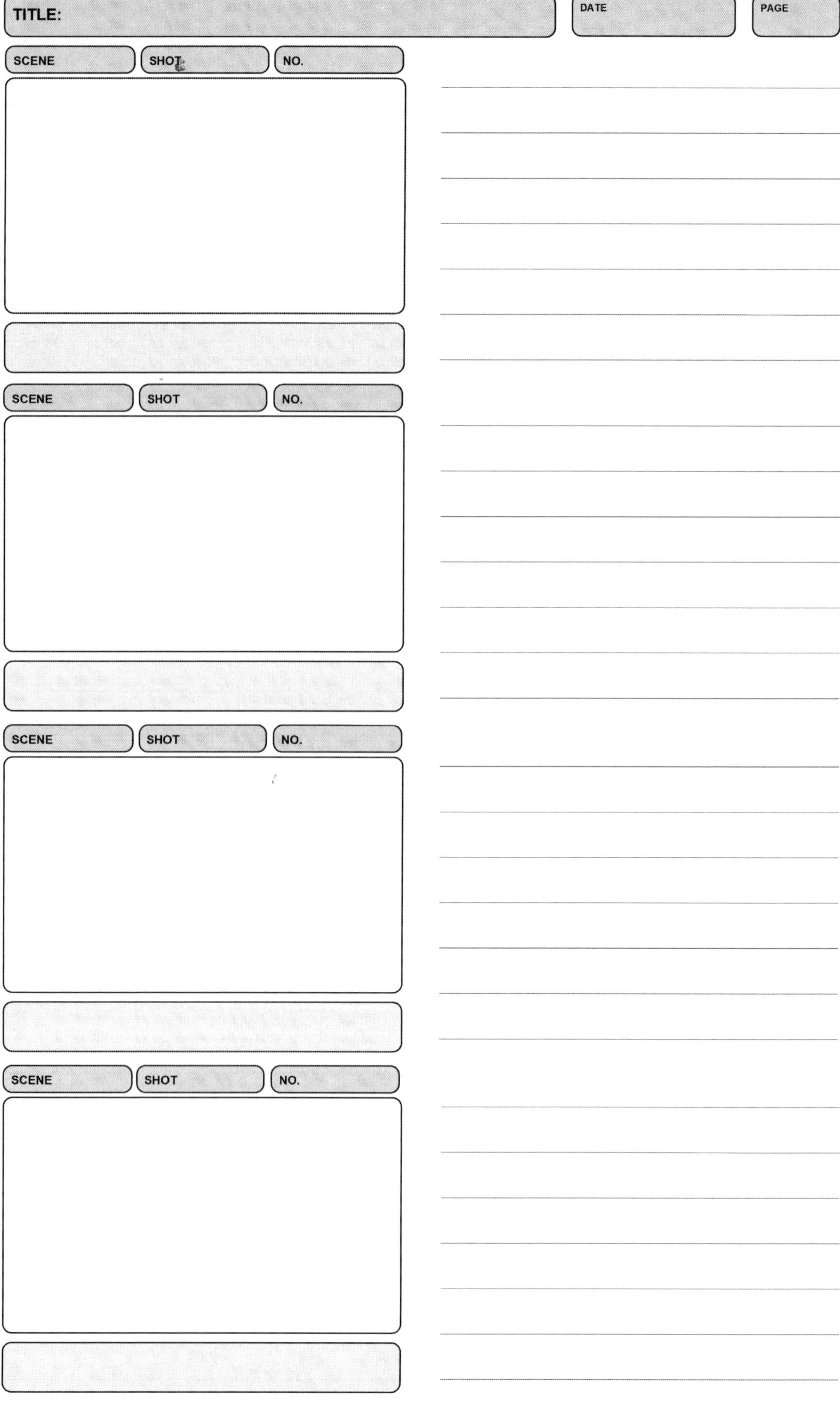

TITLE:
DATE
PAGE
SCENE   SHOT   NO.
SCENE   SHOT   NO.
SCENE   SHOT   NO.
SCENE   SHOT   NO.

TITLE: | DATE | PAGE

SCENE | SHOT | NO.

SCENE | SHOT | NO.

SCENE | SHOT | NO.

SCENE | SHOT | NO.

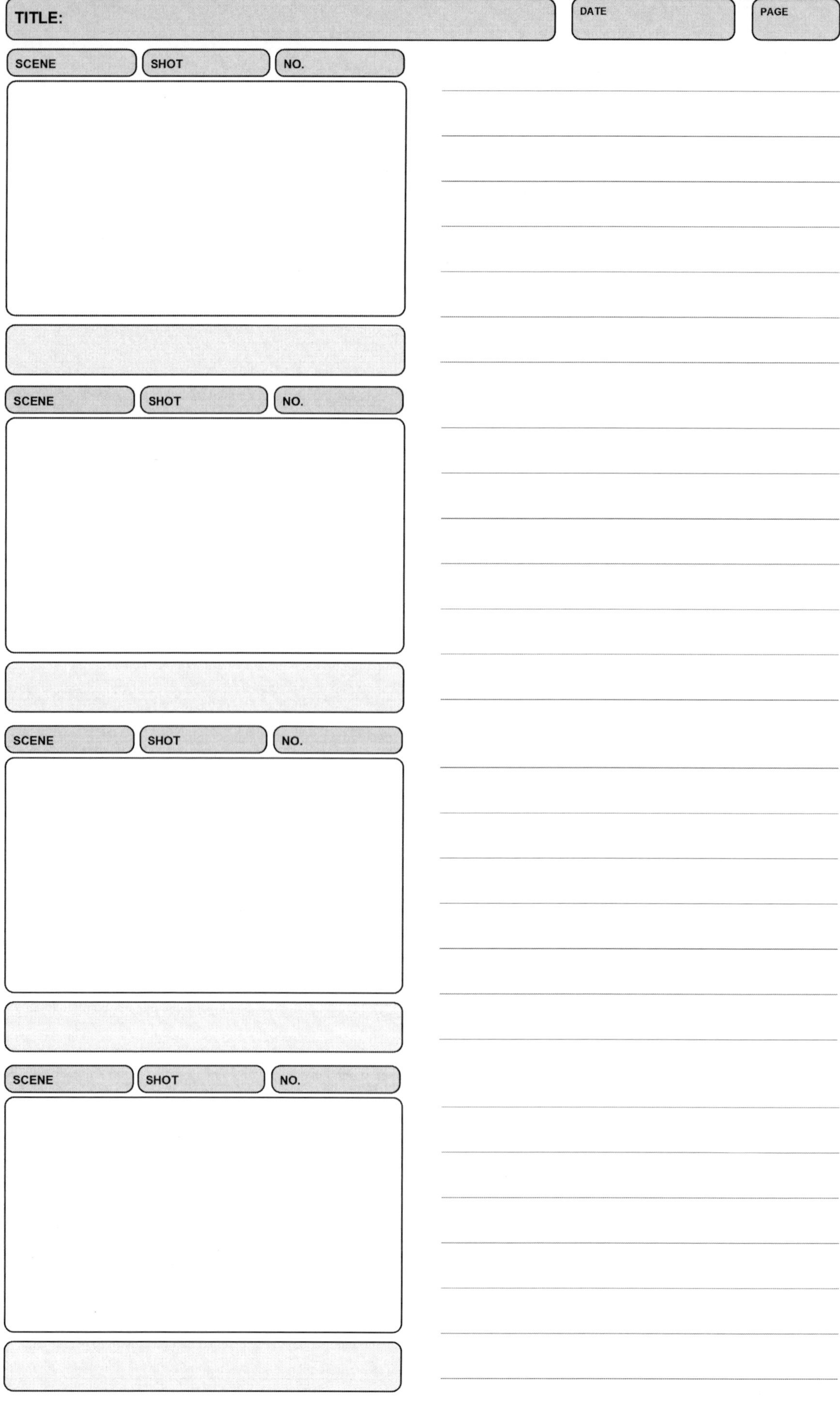

TITLE:
DATE
PAGE
SCENE
SHOT
NO.
SCENE
SHOT
NO.
SCENE
SHOT
NO.
SCENE
SHOT
NO.

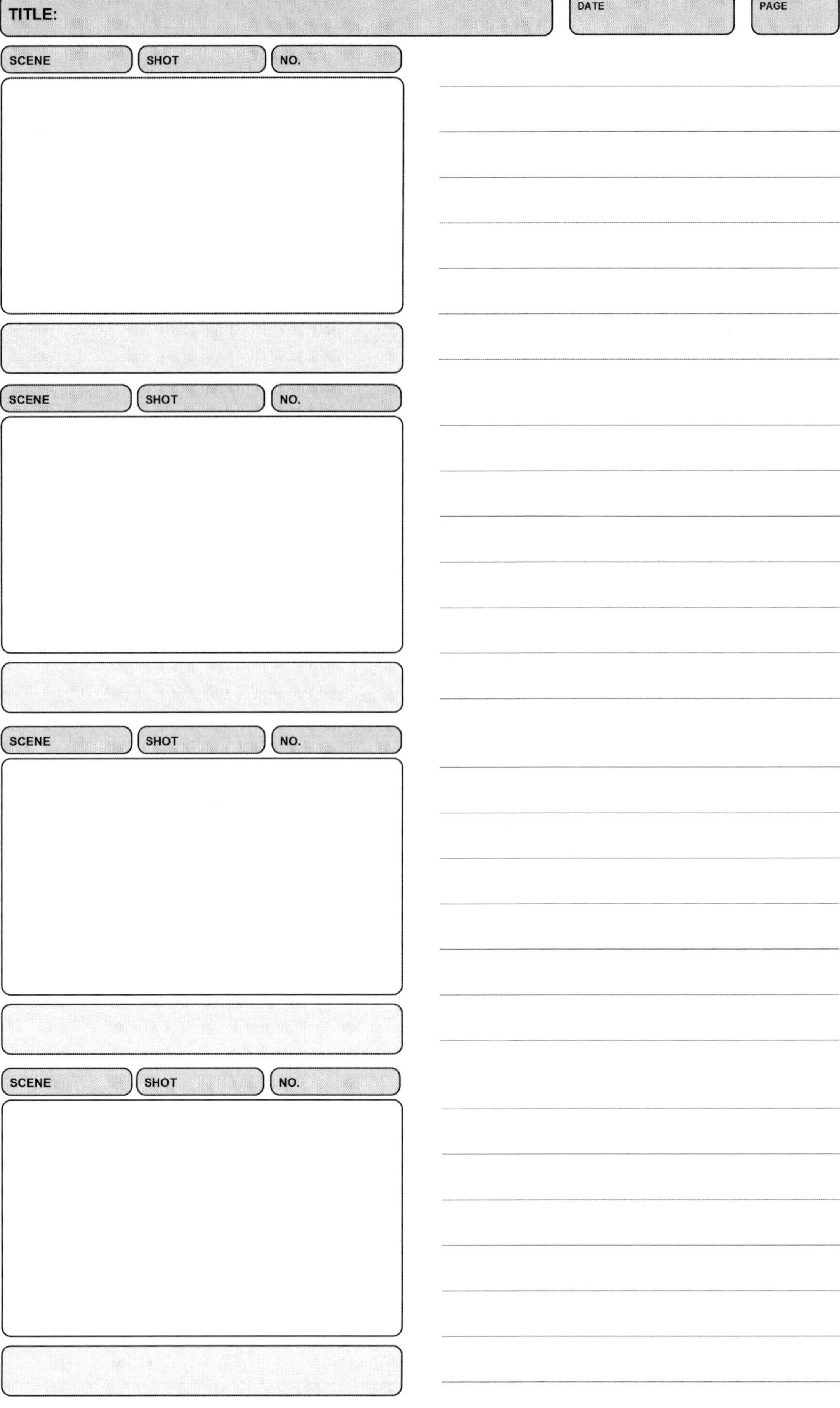

TITLE:
DATE
PAGE
SCENE
SHOT
NO.
SCENE
SHOT
NO.
SCENE
SHOT
NO.
SCENE
SHOT
NO.

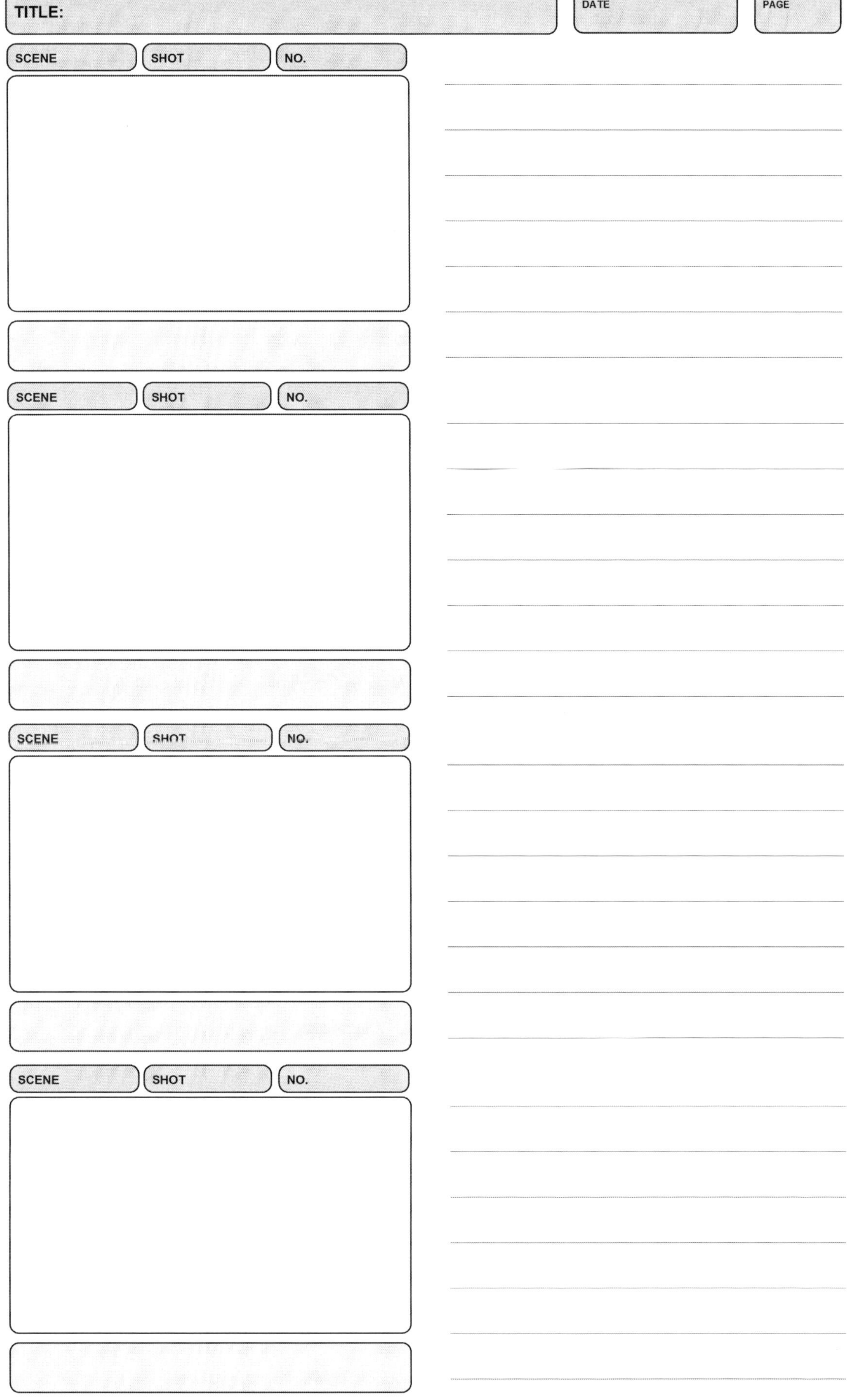

TITLE:
DATE
PAGE
SCENE
SHOT
NO.
SCENE
SHOT
NO.
SCENE
SHOT
NO.
SCENE
SHOT
NO.

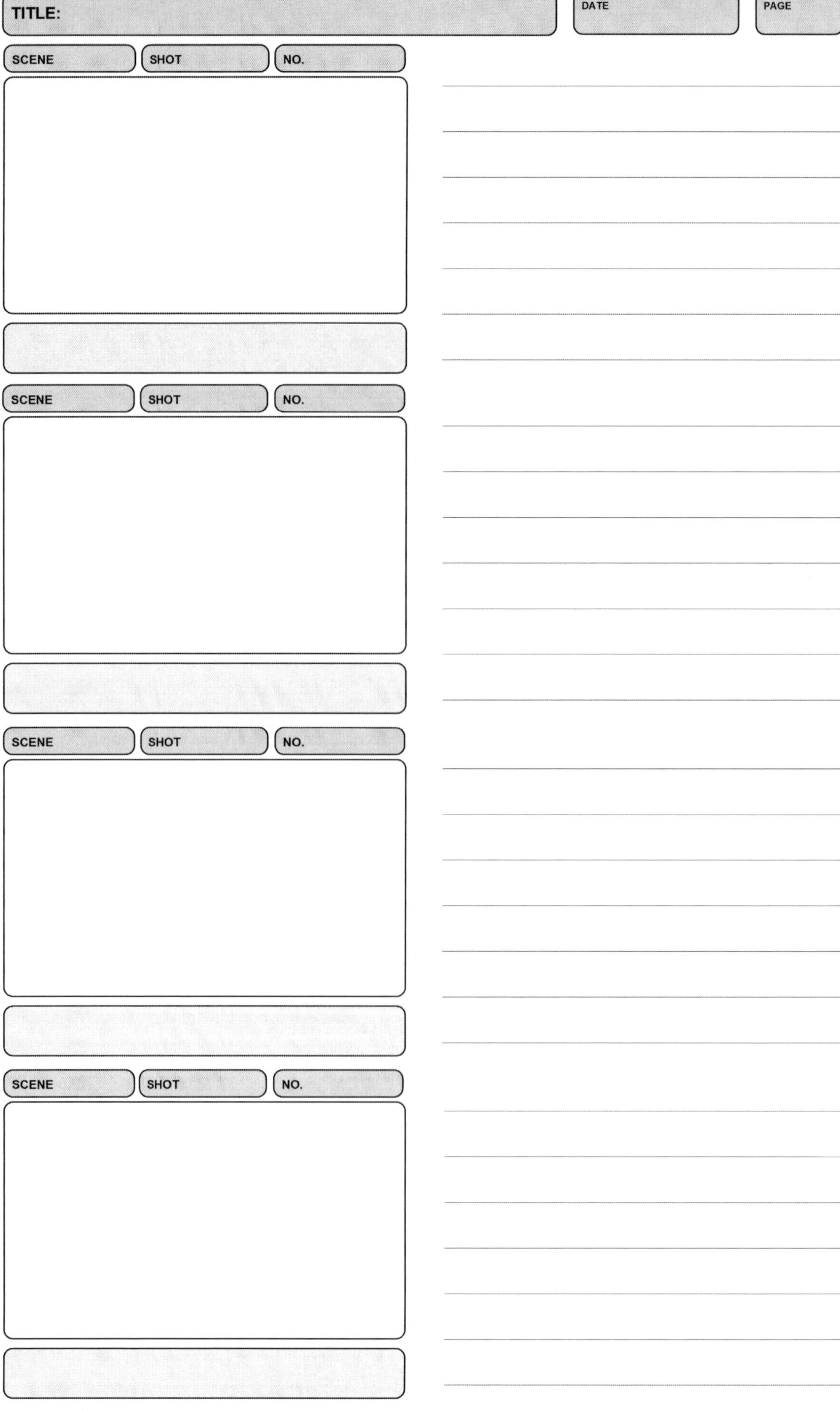
TITLE:
DATE
PAGE
SCENE
SHOT
NO.
SCENE
SHOT
NO.
SCENE
SHOT
NO.
SCENE
SHOT
NO.

TITLE:
DATE
PAGE
SCENE
SHOT
NO.
SCENE
SHOT
NO.
SCENE
SHOT
NO.
SCENE
SHOT
NO.

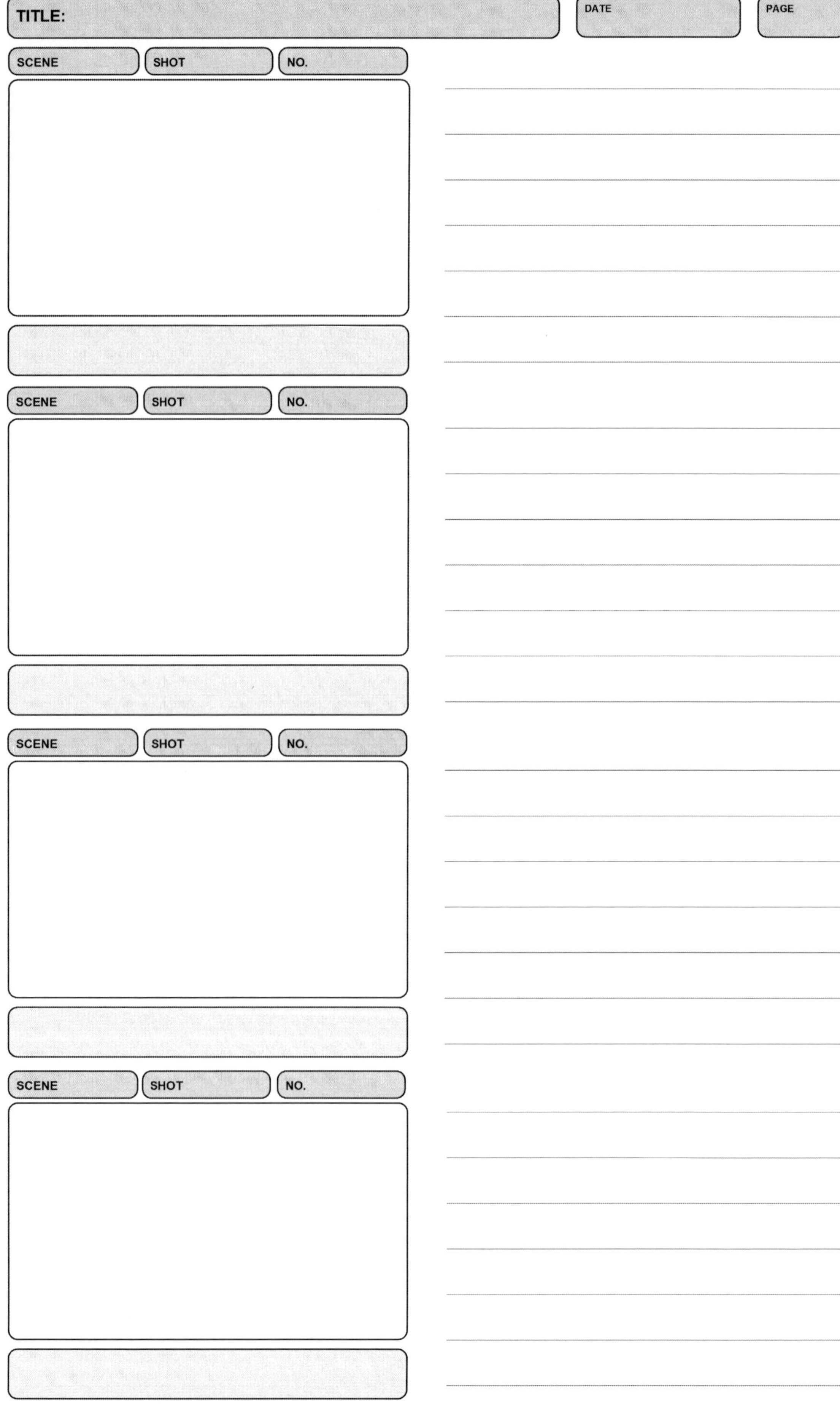

TITLE:
DATE
PAGE
SCENE
SHOT
NO.
SCENE
SHOT
NO.
SCENE
SHOT
NO.
SCENE
SHOT
NO.

DATE

PAGE

SCENE   SHOT   NO.

SCENE   SHOT   NO.

SCENE   SHOT   NO.

SCENE   SHOT   NO.

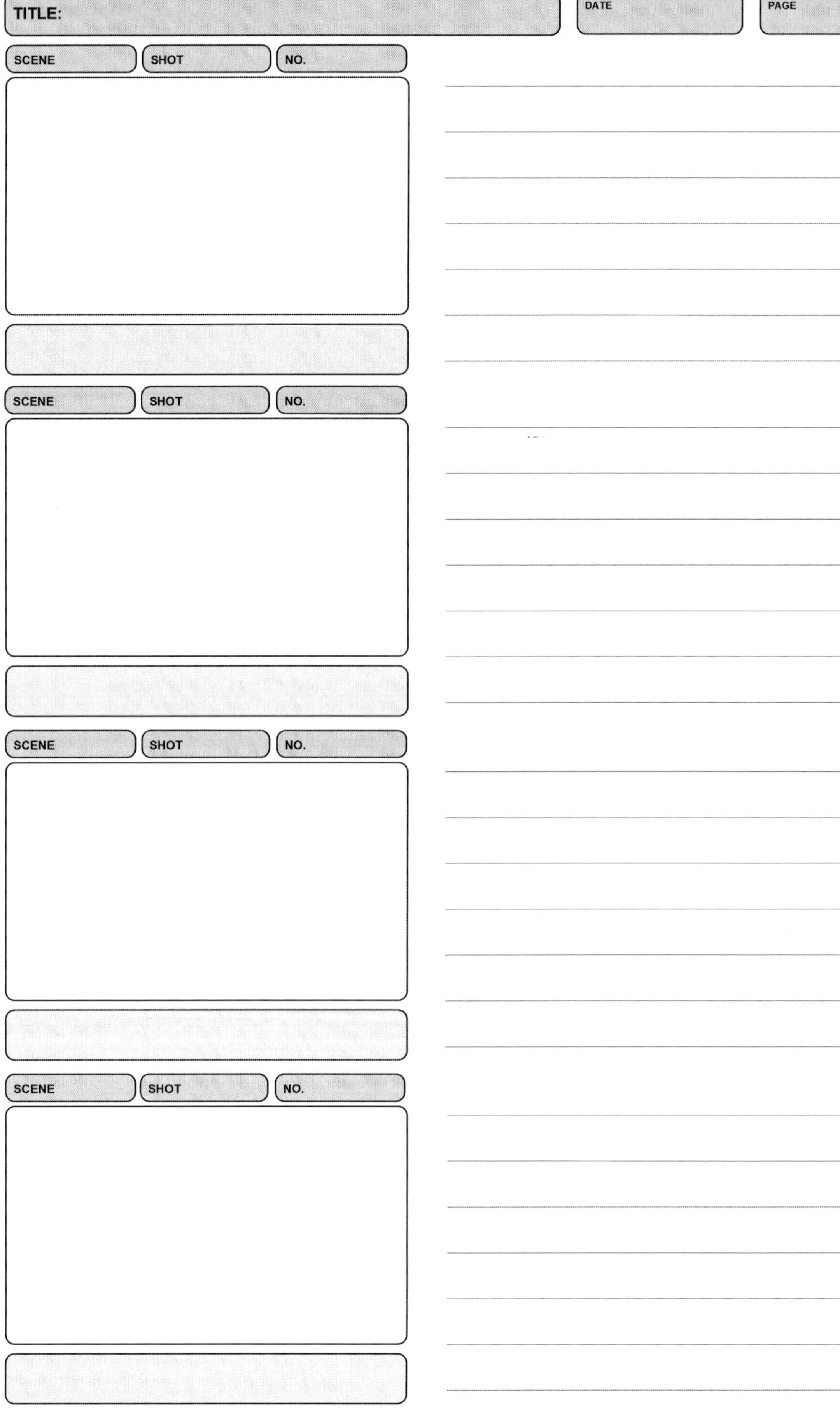
TITLE:
DATE
PAGE
SCENE
SHOT
NO.
SCENE
SHOT
NO.
SCENE
SHOT
NO.
SCENE
SHOT
NO.

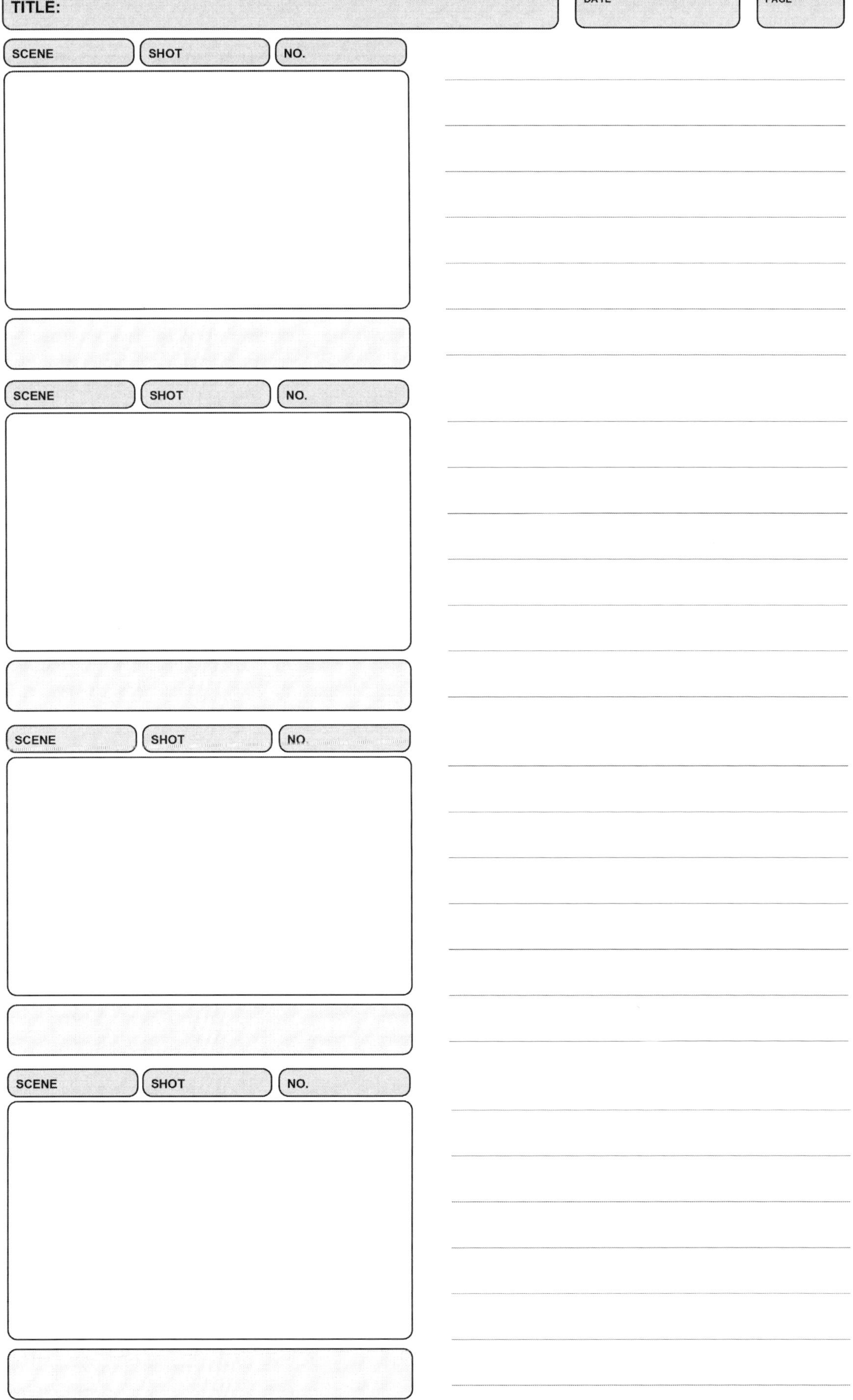

TITLE:
DATE
PAGE
SCENE
SHOT
NO.
SCENE
SHOT
NO.
SCENE
SHOT
NO.
SCENE
SHOT
NO.

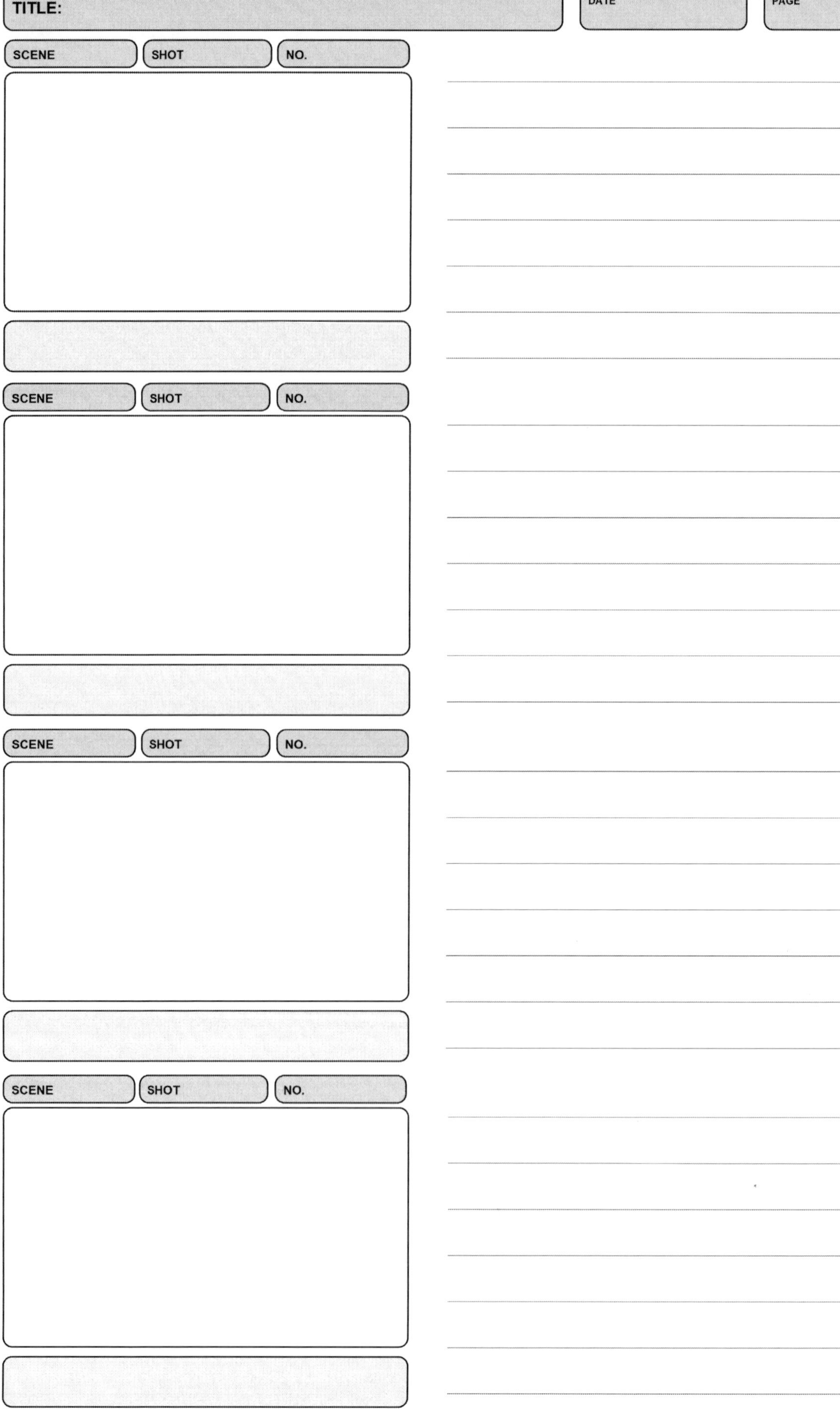

TITLE:
DATE
PAGE
SCENE
SHOT
NO.
SCENE
SHOT
NO.
SCENE
SHOT
NO.
SCENE
SHOT
NO.

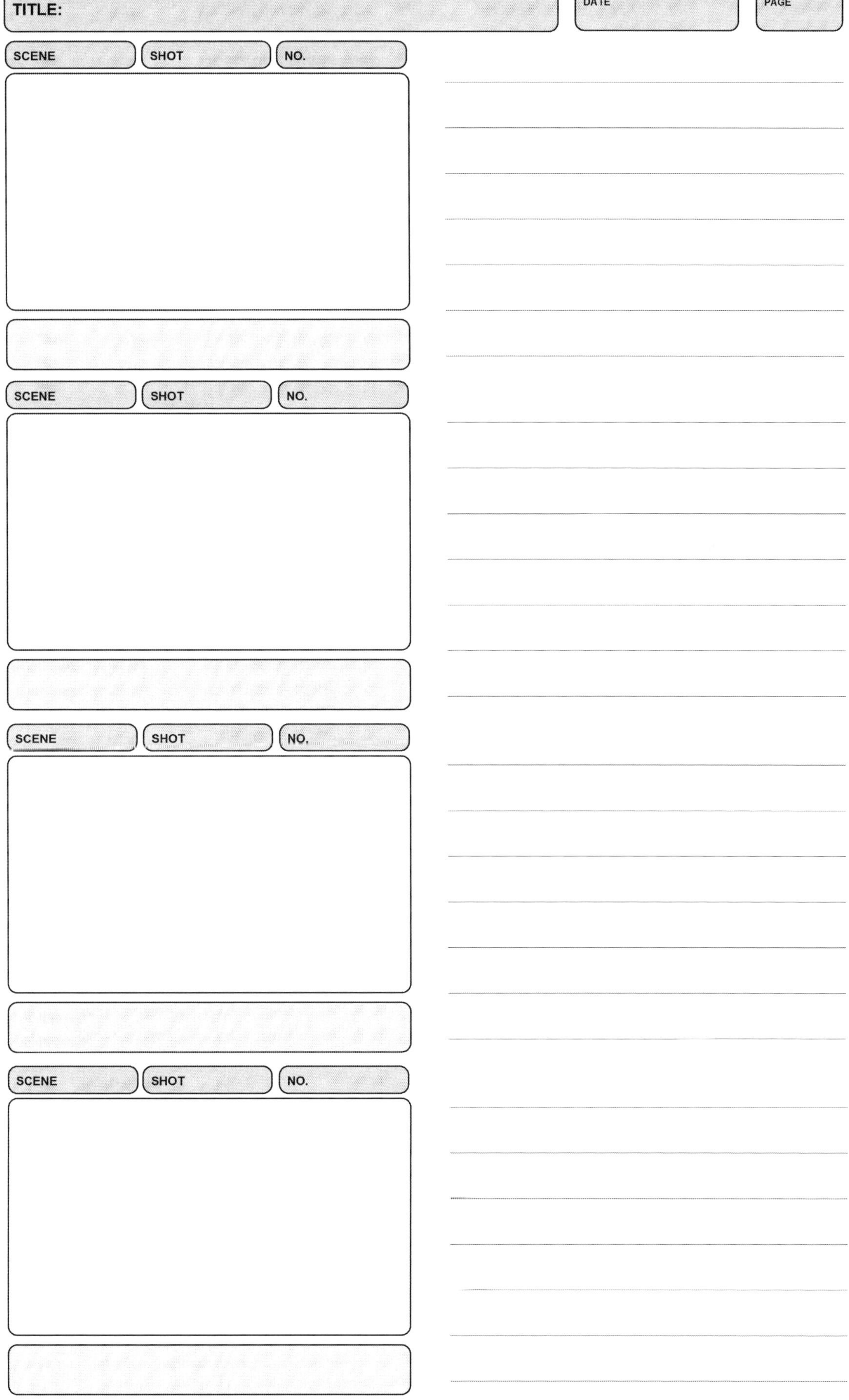

TITLE:
DATE
PAGE
SCENE
SHOT
NO.
SCENE
SHOT
NO.
SCENE
SHOT
NO.
SCENE
SHOT
NO.

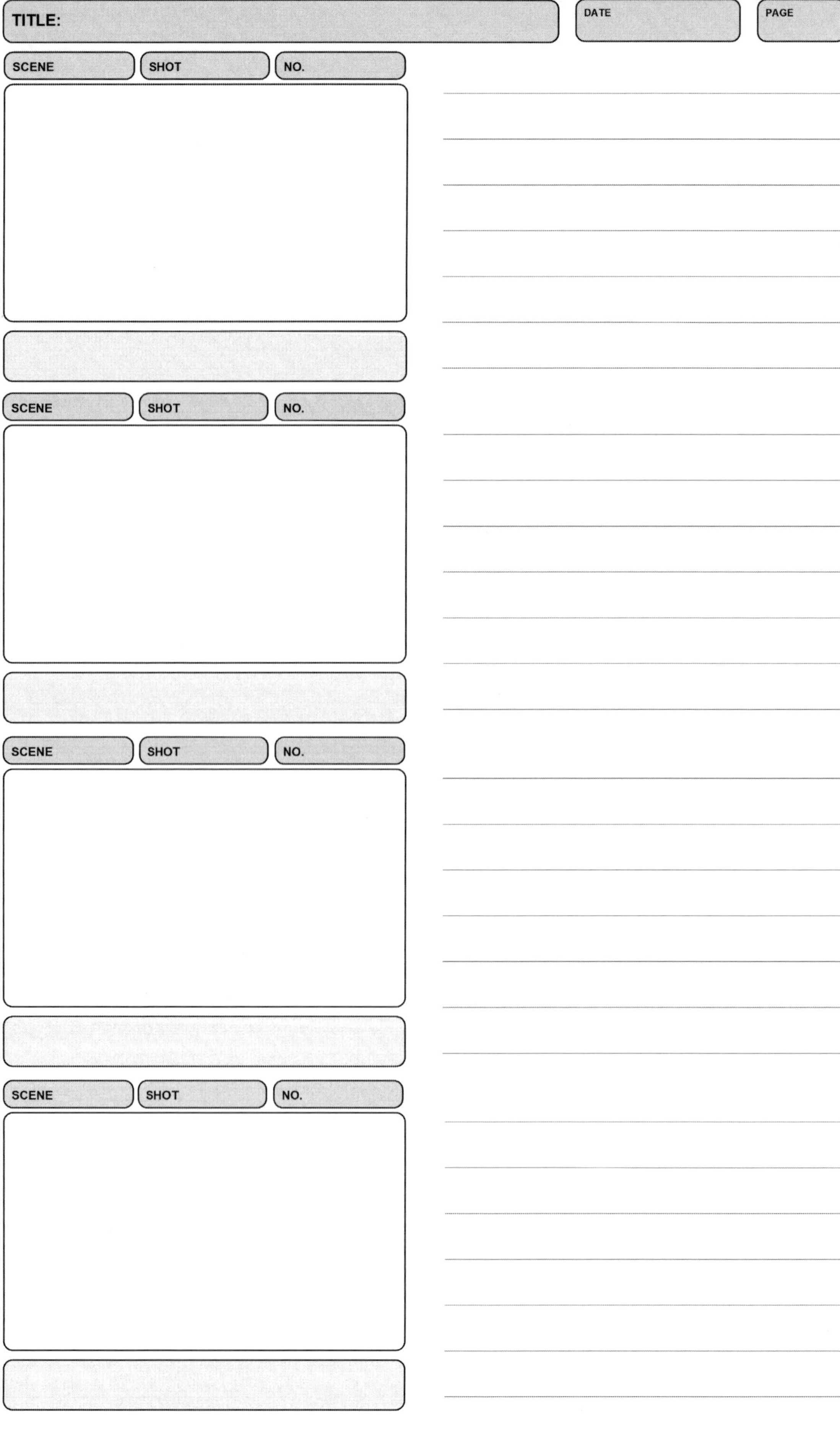

TITLE:
DATE
PAGE
SCENE
SHOT
NO.
SCENE
SHOT
NO.
SCENE
SHOT
NO.
SCENE
SHOT
NO.

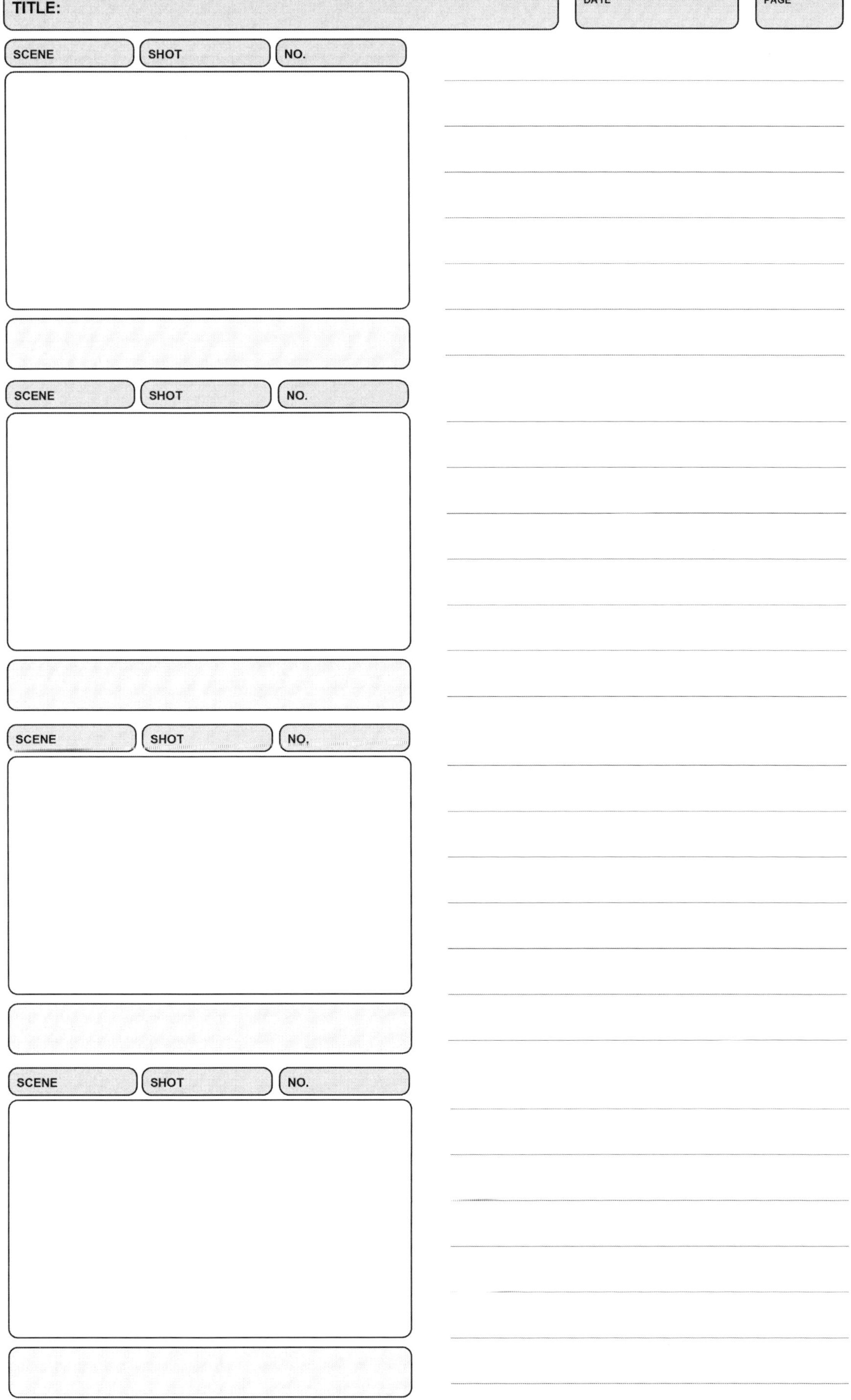

TITLE:
DATE
PAGE
SCENE
SHOT
NO.
SCENE
SHOT
NO.
SCENE
SHOT
NO,
SCENE
SHOT
NO.

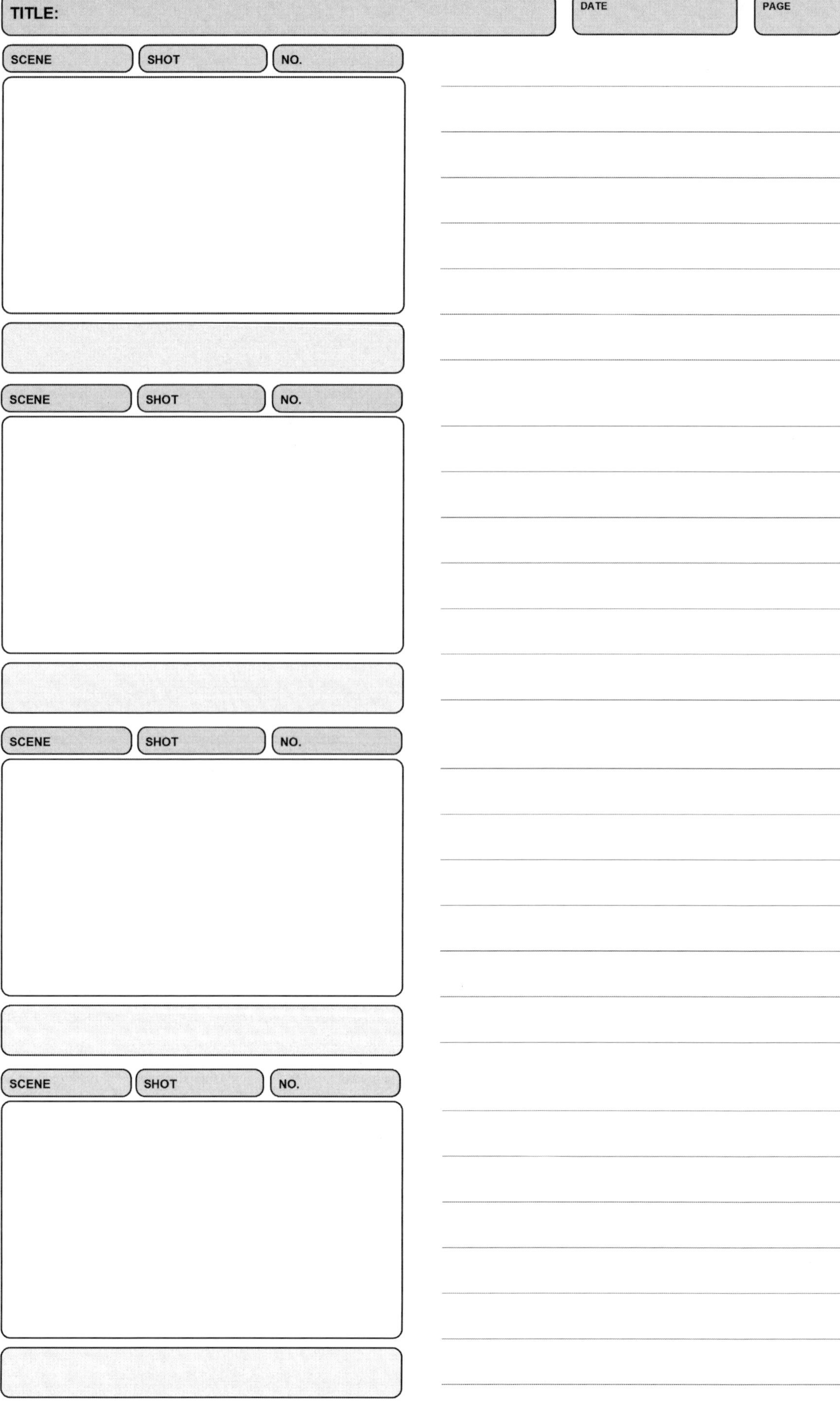

TITLE:
DATE
PAGE
SCENE
SHOT
NO.
SCENE
SHOT
NO.
SCENE
SHOT
NO.
SCENE
SHOT
NO.

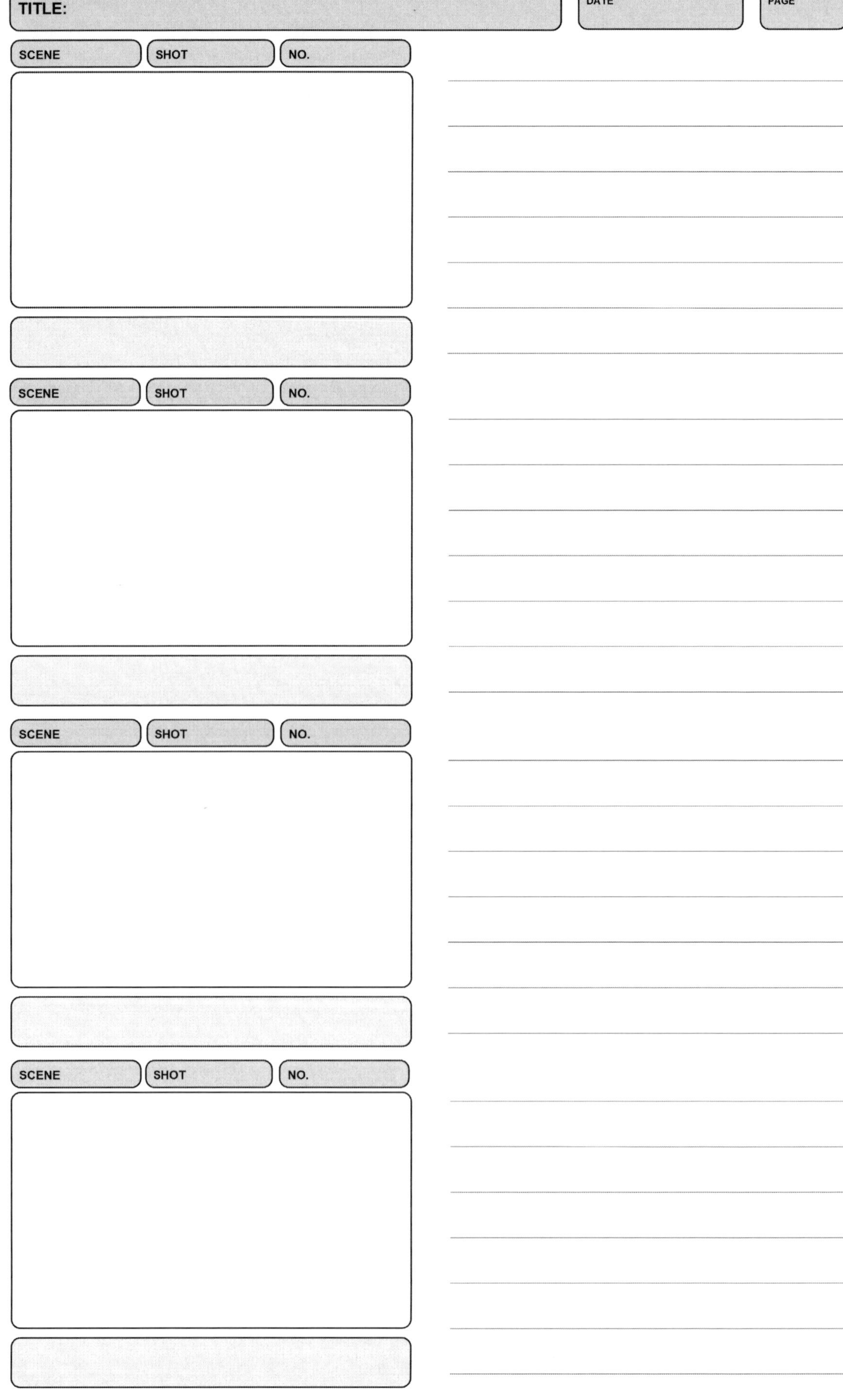

TITLE:
DATE
PAGE
SCENE
SHOT
NO.
SCENE
SHOT
NO.
SCENE
SHOT
NO.
SCENE
SHOT
NO.

TITLE:
DATE
PAGE
SCENE
SHOT
NO.
SCENE
SHOT
NO.
SCENE
SHOT
NO.
SCENE
SHOT
NO.

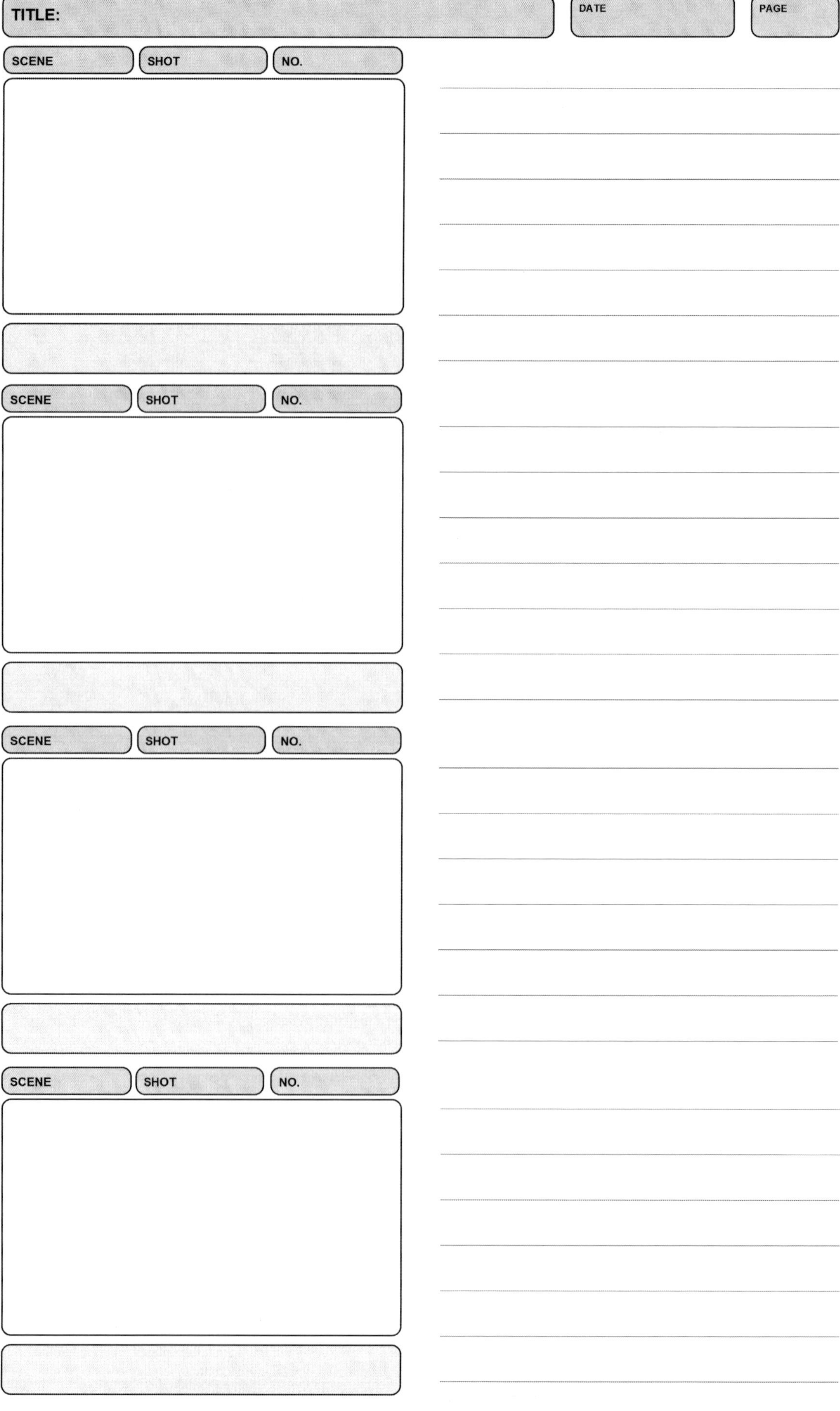

TITLE:
DATE
PAGE
SCENE
SHOT
NO.
SCENE
SHOT
NO.
SCENE
SHOT
NO.
SCENE
SHOT
NO.

SCENE   SHOT   NO.

SCENE   SHOT   NO.

SCENE   SHOT   NO.

SCENE   SHOT   NO.

Made in the USA
San Bernardino, CA
16 April 2014